How to do life!

Wisdom Nuggets from Proverbs

Caroline Bimbo Afolalu

Copyright © 2022 Caroline Bimbo Afolalu

All rights reserved

No part of this book can be reproduced in any form or by written electronic or mechanical, including photocopying, recording, or by any information retrieval system or otherwise without the prior written permission of the author or publisher.

Published by
Whitstone Books
Croydon UK
June 2022

Printed in Great Britain

Although every precaution has been taken, in the preparation of this book, the publisher and author assume no responsibility for errors or omissions. Neither is any liability assumed for damages resulting from the use of the information held herein.

ISBN 978-0-9574755-7-1

"Getting wisdom is the wisest thing you can do! And whatever else you do, develop good judgement."

PROVERBS 4:7

CONTENTS

Dedication xiii
Acknowledgements xv
Introduction xvii
Solomon's Prayer for Wisdom xviii
    The Purpose of Proverbs xix
    Wisdom Nuggets for Human Living xix

CHAPTER 1
The Fear of the Lord 1

CHAPTER 2
Obedience to Parents 6

CHAPTER 3
Do Not Yield to Bad Influence 9
Joseph and Potiphar's Wife 10
The Two Paths – Blessings and Curses 12

CHAPTER 4
Do not be Complacent or Careless 13

CHAPTER 5
Make Wisdom and Insight your Priority 16

CHAPTER 6
Trust God! Do not Assume You Know It All 18

CHAPTER 7
The Power of Love 21
The Excellence of Love 22

CHAPTER 8
Honour God with Everything you Own 24
The Widow's Gift 26
Jesus Teaching on Money and Possession 29

CHAPTER 9
The Discipline of God 30

CHAPTER 10
Wisdom is Better than Money 33

CHAPTER 11
Wisdom and Eternal Life 35

CHAPTER 12
Help Those Who Deserve a Helping Hand 37

CHAPTER 13
Maintain a Pure Heart 40

CHAPTER 14
Honest and Pure Communication 43
James' Teaching About the Tongue 45

CHAPTER 15
Focus and Moral Standard 48

CHAPTER 16
Flee Immorality 52

CHAPTER 17
Take Wise Decisions 54

CHAPTER 18
Renegotiate Bad Deals 56

CHAPTER 19
Be Organised - Work Smart! 58

CHAPTER 20
Be Diligent – Work Hard! 60

CHAPTER 21
Detestable Behaviours 62
The Seven Things God Hates 63

CHAPTER 22
A Beautiful Life for the Godly 70

CHAPTER 23
Lust and Adultery 72
Apostle Paul's Teaching About Maintaining the Integrity of Marriage .. 73
Jesus Extends Adultery to Include Lust 73

CHAPTER 24
Mercy and Forgiveness 76
The Lord's Prayer and Forgiveness 77

CHAPTER 25
Beware of Deception 79

CHAPTER 26
Godly Wealth and Riches 82
Jesus Explains Why the Worldly Gain Riches – The Parable of the
Shrewd Manager 84
The Parable of the Weeds 85

CHAPTER 27
Fear, Faith, and Positive Thinking 87
Examples of Positive Faith-Filled Prayers 89
God Gives the Spirit of Love, not of Fear 90

CHAPTER 28
Slothfulness and Laziness 92
Jesus' Teaching About Slothfulness – The Parable of the Talents 93

CHAPTER 29
Long Life 95

CHAPTER 30
Ambition and Achievement 97

CHAPTER 31
Honesty in Business 99

CHAPTER 32
Godly People and a Nation's Prosperity 101

CHAPTER 33
Give Good Work and Negotiate a Good Pay 103
Jacob Negotiated a Good Wage for His Labour 104

CHAPTER 34
Generosity – Be Generous! 105

CHAPTER 35
Trust in God, not in Riches! 108

CHAPTER 36
Do Not Exploit or Abuse Your Family 110

CHAPTER 37
The Power of Words 112

CHAPTER 38
Righteousness and a Happy Home 115

CHAPTER 39
The Integrity of Work 117

CHAPTER 40
Good People are Good to Their Animals 119
God intervened when Balaam Maltreated his Donkey 120

CHAPTER 41
Stay on the Job – Only the Witless Chase Whims and Fancies 121

CHAPTER 42
Be Teachable 123

CHAPTER 43
Emotional Intelligence – Stay Calm! 125

CHAPTER 44
Truth and Keeping Promises 127

CHAPTER 45
Listen to Godly Advice 129

CHAPTER 46
Parental Discipline 131

CHAPTER 47
Wisdom and Building a Successful Home 134
The Way of Love - The Fruit of the Holy Spirit 136
God's Blessing Upon the Family that Live in Unity 136

CHAPTER 48
Be An Instrument of Peace – A Gentle Answer Diffuses Anger 137
Nabal's Foolish Words 138
David's Anger 138
Abigail's Intercession and Calming Words 139
Abigail's thoughtful words diffuse David's anger 140

CHAPTER 49
Genuine Prayers Triumphs Hypocrisy 142

CHAPTER 50
Optimism, Hope, Joy, and a Cheerful Heart 144
The Serenity of the Shunammite Woman 146

CHAPTER 51
Seek Good Counsel to Succeed 148

CHAPTER 52
Appropriate Answers and Timely Word 150

CHAPTER 53
Peace With Enemies 153

CHAPTER 54
Commit Your Plans to God 156

CHAPTER 55
Do Not Gloat Over Misfortune 159

CHAPTER 56
Loyalty in Relationships 161
Ruth's Loyalty to Naomi 162

CHAPTER 57
There is Power and Protection in God's Names 164

CHAPTER 58
The Act of Listening Before Speaking 166

CHAPTER 59
The Power of Motivation and a Healthy Spirit 168

CHAPTER 60
The Power of Gifts 171

CHAPTER 61
Marriage and Finding a Good Spouse 174

CHAPTER 62
Oversleep and Poverty..178

CHAPTER 63
Hold on to Collateral on Loans...180

CHAPTER 64
Do Honest Work - Stealing and Fraud Has Consequences.....182

CHAPTER 65
Planning, Expert Advice and Alliances......................................185

CHAPTER 66
Secrets and Confidentiality 187

CHAPTER 67
Honour Your Parents...189

CHAPTER 68
Divine Direction and God's Guidance 191

CHAPTER 69
Preparation and Victory..194

CHAPTER 70
Be Skilled at Your Work, Skilled Workers are Always in Demand.........197

CHAPTER 71
Do Not Wear Yourself Out Trying to Get Rich 200

CHAPTER 72
Moderation of Food and Wine... 203

CHAPTER 73
Intelligence and Wise Strategies 205

CHAPTER 74
Stay Upright - Do Not Compromise 207

CHAPTER 75
Subdue Yourself - Self-Discipline 209

CHAPTER 76
Teamwork and Friendships 211

CHAPTER 77
Vision, Purpose, and Revelation 213

CHAPTER 78
Humility Versus Pride 216

CHAPTER 79
Managing Negative Criticisms 219

CHAPTER 80
Get Rid of Negative Emotions 221

CHAPTER 81
An Excellent Wife 223
The Wife of Noble Character 223
The Qualities of a Good Wife 224

Conclusion – True Prosperity 227
Altar Call – Prayer of Salvation 229
    Prayer of Salvation, Author's Version 229
    Welcome Letter to new Christians 230
    New Christian To-Do List: 230
About the Author 231
Other Books by the Author 233
Contact Details 235
Works Cited 237
Recommended Resources 239

DEDICATION

I humbly dedicate this book to God the Father, God the Son -Jesus Christ, and God the Holy Spirit, for the divine gift of teaching and wisdom.

ACKNOWLEDGEMENTS

- Appreciation to all my family, friends, Beautiful Foods Ltd customers, work colleagues, church family and family in-laws, who have shown me exceptional love over the years.
- Special thanks to my confidants Julie Park and Thelma Egunjobi.
- A big thank you to my amazing daughter Grace Ife Afolalu, and my wonderful sons Bisi and Pelumi Afolalu.
- Massive thank you to my husband, Tunde Afolalu, just like Paul and Apollos, I plant, he waters but it is God who gives us the increase.

To God be all the Glory!

"I planted the seed, Apollos watered it, but God has been making it grow."

1 CORINTHIANS 3:6

INTRODUCTION

The purpose of this book is to examine the wisdom that is useful for living a great, prosperous, healthy, and successful life both physically and spiritually. First, what is wisdom? Wisdom is the quality of being wise, with experience, knowledge, and good judgement. It is the act of acquiring knowledge with the ability to make beneficial use of gained knowledge by applying the knowledge effectively to life circumstances.

The spiritual realm controls the physical world, so it is wise to live a life based upon the foundational truth taught in the word of God, the Bible. This Book will, therefore, focus on the important scriptures written by King Solomon, the author of the Book of Proverbs. His wisdom, if diligently followed will create a successful life.

Everything in the world and our physical realm originates from the spirit realm, it is from there, that God created the universe and everything there is. Therefore, human beings can create for themselves a good and successful long life in good health and prosperity by adhering to the wisdom provided in the word of God which informs our world of the will and purposes of God the creator.

Knowing God first, then applying his divine principles to how one does life, receiving help from the supernatural realm, will result in a beautiful and satisfying life. The knowledge for living life successfully is in the instruction booklet of life, the Bible.

However, this book will narrow down on the wisdom tips provided by King Solomon in the Book of Proverbs. The Book of Proverbs is full of wisdom and tips for a successful living. The criteria for doing well in life are the fear of God and obedience to God's commandments documented in the word of God.

King Solomon, a respected king was the wealthiest, and wisest man on earth during his reign as the king of Israel. He used the Book of Proverbs as a means of documenting his insights on how to do life, offering wise tips in his writings. He offers his readers advice on how to do life wisely and successfully.

Solomon's life experience teaches Believers, that God is the source of wisdom. King Solomon asked God for the gift of wisdom to rule his nation and God granted his wishes.

Solomon's Prayer for Wisdom

"Give me wisdom and knowledge, so that I may go out and come in [performing my duties] before this people, for [otherwise] who can rule *and* administer justice to this great people of Yours? God replied to Solomon, "Because this was in your heart and you did not ask for riches, possessions or honour *and* personal glory, or the life of those who hate you, nor have you even asked for long life, but you have asked for wisdom and knowledge for yourself so that you may rule *and* administer justice to My people over whom I have made you king, wisdom and knowledge have been granted you. I will also give you riches, possessions, and honour, such as none of the kings who were before you have possessed nor will those who will come after you."

2 CHRONICLES 1:10-13

One may ask what is the purpose of wisdom? Solomon made a list of the key benefits of gaining wisdom in the Book of Proverbs.

The Purpose of Proverbs

These are the proverbs of Solomon, David's son, king of Israel. Their purpose is:

- To teach people wisdom and discipline.
- To help them understand the insights of the wise.
- To teach people to live disciplined and successful lives.
- To help them do what is right, just, and fair.
- These proverbs will give insight into the simple.
- Knowledge and discernment to the young.
- Let the wise listen to these proverbs and become even wiser.
- Let those with understanding receive guidance.
- To encourage the fear of the LORD which is the foundation of true knowledge.

Proverbs 1:1-7

There are useful lessons for living a good life in the Book of Proverbs. I aim to point out to the readers, the key wisdom nuggets that can resolve the riddles of life as compiled in the Book of Proverbs. King Solomon provides wise instructions for the spiritual, financial, physical, and moral growth of his readers. His insights teach the young person how to live with specific instructions to help live the good life. It covers vital areas of human living.

Wisdom Nuggets for Human Living

- Righteousness and Peace
- Justice and Integrity
- Success and Prosperity
- Happiness and Health
- Shrewdness to the inexperience
- Knowledge and Discretion

Wisdom protects people; it helps the people of God live a fantastic and exuberant life. It is important to mention that keeping the word of God will protect people from sin and bad lifestyle which in turn offer the benefits of long life, prosperity, and peace to everyone who follows the wisdom of Solomon.

The question is how does one obtain wisdom? Wisdom is in the word of God, the Bible, so, those who desire wisdom have the option of either asking God in prayer or reading the Bible to glean wisdom directly from the word of God through the revelation of God the Holy Spirit.

Reading and meditating on the word of God, combined with prayer for God's enlightenment, give an advantage to the Believer and help them progress in their life's journey. God advised Joshua to read and meditate on the word of God by which he will be successful. So, it is safe to say that the Bible contains the wisdom necessary for a successful life.

> **"Study this Book of Instruction continually. Meditate on it day and night so you will be sure to obey everything written in it. Only then will you prosper and succeed in all you do."**
>
> JOSHUA 1:8

It is essential to mention that wisdom is not an elusive or an abstract concept that is difficult to grasp or understand as it can sometimes appear to be. It is a set of divine rules and principles for living, written in the scriptures with which the Believer may live an upright and wonderful life if followed diligently. The good news is, therefore, that people who lack wisdom can ask God in prayer or read the Bible for wise instructions.

> **"If any of you lacks wisdom, you should ask God, who gives generously to all without finding fault, and it will be given to you."**
>
> JAMES 1:5

.However, one must mention the fact that there are two types of wisdom. Christians need to learn to distinguish between the two types. There is godly wisdom from heaven and worldly craftiness from the world. James wrote in his Book, that the wisdom from heaven is peaceful and good. It is different from the wisdom of the world which is selfishness and crafty living.

> "But the wisdom from above is first pure [morally and spiritually undefiled], then peace-loving [courteous, considerate], gentle, reasonable [and willing to listen], full of compassion and good fruits. It is unwavering, without [self-righteous] hypocrisy [and self-serving guile]."
>
> JAMES 3:17

PRAYER

Father, the giver of all things, we ask for wisdom from above to live successfully in Jesus' name. Amen

CHAPTER 1

The Fear of the Lord

> *"The fear of the LORD is the foundation of true knowledge, but fools despise wisdom and discipline."*
>
> PROVERBS 1:7

The Bible says the fear of the Lord is the beginning of knowledge because the realisation of God's awesomeness means one knows and fully understands the basic commandments necessary to fulfil his expectation from humanity. Therefore, the understanding of his word, the Bible is the foundation of knowledge and understanding which is wisdom.

The Believer's knowledge of the word coupled with its application gives the reward of a beautiful life. The word of God recommends obedience to the word which makes a person or a nation wise.

> **"Obey them completely, and you will display your wisdom and intelligence among the surrounding nations. When they hear all these decrees, they will exclaim, 'How wise and prudent are the people of this great nation!"**
>
> DEUTERONOMY 4:6

The wisdom nugget is to learn the word of God and observe his instructions. Simply put, it means to be a doer of the word and to physically take actions based on the guidance of God's word. This demands the obedience and commitment of the Believer. James advised Believers to be committed to following God's teaching with action, otherwise one will be deluding oneself and such a person's religion will be a sham.

> "But prove yourselves doers of the word [actively and continually obeying God's precepts], and not merely listeners [who hear the word but fail to internalize its meaning], deluding yourselves [by unsound reasoning contrary to the truth]."
>
> JAMES 1:22

Fulfilling the will of God determines how well a person can live above evil and the various temptations of life. Obedience of the word of God places the Believer and doer of the word above evil and ahead in life. It offers prosperity to the soul, body, and spirit. God advised Joshua to learn his word and live a life fully devoted to God.

> "Be strong and very courageous. Be careful to obey all the instructions Moses gave you. Do not deviate from them, turning either to the right or to the left. Then you will be successful in everything you do to meditate on the word of God. Study this Book of Instruction continually. Meditate on it day and night so you will be sure to obey everything written in it. Only then will you prosper and succeed in all you do."
>
> JOSHUA 1:7-8

The word of God is the written word, the Bible, or the person of his son Jesus Christ. Therefore, Christians are to live their lives in obedience to the written word and the examples provided by Jesus Christ. They should seek the help of the Holy Spirit whom Jesus prayed will guide them into righteousness to enjoy a good life and enter the kingdom of God.

> "And I will ask the Father and he will give you another Advocate, who will never leave you. He is the Holy Spirit, who leads into

> **all truth. The world cannot receive him because it isn't looking for him and doesn't recognize him. But you know him because he lives with you now and later will be in you."**
>
> JOHN 14:16-17

The Holy Spirit reveals the truth of God to the Believer and offers an understanding of the word and the ways of God. The instruction to learn and obey the word of God is important for every Christian and anyone who aspires to live a prosperous life in the world.

Inspirational and Motivational speakers often draw their quotations and teachings from the word of God. Though they may not acknowledge God in truth and Spirit, they can still benefit from the usefulness and the application of his word, and the necessary wisdom required for a successful life.

It is important to establish the fact that God is not a respecter of person. Whatever he promised in his word will happen in the lives of anyone who believes in his word. Therefore, people who do not know God personally as their Lord and Saviour but learn his laws and carry them out in life situations will prosper regardless of their spiritual status. The principles of God will work for anyone who practises the wisdom of his word.

However, such a person needs to believe and confess Jesus as their Lord and saviour to gain eternity. Whilst a person may become successful and rich with the application of the principles of the word of God, they will miss heaven if they fail to acknowledge him as God. No one can see God unless they acknowledge and accept him as God and believe in his Son Jesus Christ as the Messiah.

> **"Work at living in peace with everyone, and work at living a holy life, for those who are not holy will not see the Lord."**
>
> HEBREWS 12:14

On the other hand, whilst Christians get to make heaven and have eternal life after death, they may fall short of God's goodness and live life as utter failures if they fail to apply the word of God to life circumstances. Prosperity is, therefore, dependent on obedience to the word of God, especially his wealth and success principles.

> **"Therefore, obey the terms of this covenant so that you will prosper in everything you do."**
>
> DEUTERONOMY 29:9

Learning, understanding, and obeying the word of God is the key to a prosperous life. The knowledge of God's word gives the Believer courage and confidence to take the necessary actions, knowing without a doubt that God will help them prosper. John prayed for Believers to prosper emotionally, financially, and spiritually.

> **"Beloved, I pray that in every way you may succeed *and* prosper and be in good health [physically], just as [I know] your soul prospers [spiritually]."**
>
> 3 JOHN 1:2

Believers, therefore, need a combination of physical and spiritual success to be happy and fulfilled Christians. Prophet Isaiah and Jesus criticised Believers who just follow God with their mouths and not their hearts.

> **"You hypocrites! Isaiah was right when he prophesied about you, for he wrote, these people honour me with their lips, but their heart is far from me. Their worship is a farce, for they teach fabricated ideas as commands from God. Then Jesus called to the crowd to come and hear. "Listen," he said, "and try to understand."**
>
> MATTHEW 15:7-10

The above kind of lifestyle will only get the Believer an empty or half a life from God. Jesus declared he has come, so, the people of God may have life and have it more abundantly, with nothing broken or missing, an abundant life (John 10:10). This simply means following God's teaching will give the Believer a full, satisfying, happy and fulfilled life.

His teaching is the beginning and the foundation upon which Christians should base their faith, in it, there is the reward of the joy of blessedness. The Book of Psalms stated the blessedness enjoyed by those who do life following God's plan for their lives, obeying his will, teaching, and counsel. Walking with God and doing life according to his word gives the Believer overflowing joy and peace.

> **"Oh, the joys of those who do not follow the advice of the wicked, or stand around with sinners, or join in with mockers but they delight in the law of the LORD, meditating on it day and night. They are like trees planted along the riverbank, bearing fruit each season. Their leaves never wither, and they prosper in all they do."**
>
> PSALM 1:1-3

PRAYER

Dear Lord, we pray for wisdom which is the foundation for building a good life in Jesus' name. Amen.

CHAPTER 2

Obedience to Parents

> "My child, listen when your father corrects you.
> Do not neglect your mother's instruction."
>
> PROVERBS 1:8

A parent is a person that stands in the position of parenting a child. It could be the biological father, mother, adopted parents or anyone in sole authority over a child's upbringing. For certain children, this could be their grandparents, uncles, aunties, or foster parents. Whoever takes the responsibility of taking care of a child has the duty of teaching that child right from wrong.

In a Christian home, parents should teach their children the way of the Lord, so that, when they grow up, they will become upright and become people of high moral standard. Parents expect their children to do well, so teaching them to listen to sound teaching and to obey godly guidance is paramount to their success. The Bible encourages children to listen to correction and to follow the godly instructions of their parents.

> "Children, obey your parents because you belong to the Lord, for this is the right thing to do."
>
> EPHESIANS 6:1

> "Listen, my sons, to a father's instruction; pay attention and gain understanding."
>
> PROVERBS 4:1

> "My son, obey your father's commands, and don't neglect your mother's instruction."
>
> PROVERBS 6:20

The Bible encourages children to be obedient to their parents or caretakers. The wisdom of parents is meant to help a child develop understanding and wisdom to live a good and successful life. Parents owe their children godly wisdom. Failure to guide and direct children on the right path results in their ruin or destruction.

A notable example is the sons of Eli, a priest in the Bible time whose sons were undisciplined. They were disrespectful to God and behaved badly, so, God punished them.

> **"On that day I will carry out against Eli everything that I have spoken concerning his house (family), from beginning to end.**
>
> **Now I have told him that I am about to judge his house forever for the sinful behaviour which he knew [was happening] because his sons were bringing a curse on themselves [dishonouring and blaspheming God] and he did not rebuke them.**
>
> 1 SAMUEL 3:12-13

Eli failed in his duty as a father to teach his sons the way of the Lord, he did not restrain, correct, or control their excessive behaviour so they took the Lord's offerings, blasphemed God, and abused the people under their authority when they became priests.

The lesson from Eli's situation is to instruct one's children and never neglect the duty to love and discipline them. Discipline is part of parental love and responsibility. God the Father disciplines his children and corrects his people.

> "And have you forgotten the encouraging words God spoke to you as his children? He said, "My child, do not make light of the LORD's discipline, and do not give up when he corrects you. For the LORD disciplines those he loves, and he punishes each one he accepts as his child."
>
> HEBREWS 12:5-6

The wisdom that comes from parents is beautiful and honourable. Proverbs 1:9 describes it as a graceful garland for the son's head and pendants for his neck. A garland is a wreath of flowers and leaves worn on the head or hung as a decoration. It symbolises beauty and splendour. Therefore, a child who listens to and follows their parent's godly teaching will live a long, happy, and successful life.

> "Honour your father and mother. Then you will live a long and full life in the land the LORD your God is giving you."
>
> EXODUS 20:12

Instructing a child has advantages and benefits for both parents and their children. From the preceding scripture, children get the fullness of life which means long life. And parents enjoy peace of mind because once their children grow up, they will not depart from the godly way imparted to them.

> "Direct your children onto the right path, and when they are older, they will not leave it."
>
> PROVERBS 22:6

PRAYER

Father, we thank you for children all over the world, we ask for grace for parents and those in authority over children so they can guide their children in the right direction in Jesus' name. Amen.

CHAPTER 3

Do Not Yield to Bad Influence

> "My child, if sinners entice you, turn your back on them!"
>
> PROVERBS 1:10

The wisdom nugget is not to yield to bad influence. People, particularly children and young people can succumb to peer pressure and bad influence. Bad or negative people with bad character and behaviour can derail good destinies. They like to share evil and persuade others to join in their indulgencies and sin.

Believers should, therefore, protect themselves from bad associations with evildoers, otherwise, they will lead them to do wrong. The Bible teaches people to flee from evil by avoiding the gathering of those who do wickedly (Psalm 1). And Apostle Paul warns against the deceit of evildoers.

> "Let no one deceive you with empty words, for because of these things the wrath of God comes upon the sons of disobedience. Therefore, do not be partakers with them; for you were formerly darkness, but now you are Light in the Lord; walk as children of Light (for the fruit of the Light *consists* in all goodness, righteousness, and truth), trying to learn what is

pleasing to the Lord. Do not participate in the unfruitful deeds of darkness, but instead even expose them; for it is disgraceful even to speak of the things which are done by them in secret. But all things become visible when they are exposed by the light, for everything that becomes visible is light."

EPHESIANS 5:6-13

The Bible warns Believers of the folly of thinking that evil behaviour in darkness, will not become known. It states evil will eventually become known and there will be consequences. So, how does the Believer keep from evil or sinning against God in their journey of life, especially from temptations? Joseph in the Book of Genesis had a great strategy for escaping temptation and sin.

His method was to physically flee from evil. His example shows the Believer, to physically run from places or people that can lure them into wrongdoing. He had an encounter with his master Potiphar's wife, a temptress who wanted to seduce him. Being a wise young man, he fled from her bedroom to safety, thereby overcoming her temptation that would have caused him to commit adultery.

Joseph and Potiphar's Wife

"Although Potiphar's wife spoke to Joseph, day after day, he refused to go to bed with her or even be near her. One day, however, Joseph went into the house to attend to his work, and not a single household servant was inside. She grabbed Joseph by his cloak and said, "Sleep with me!" But leaving his cloak in her hand, he escaped and ran outside"

GENESIS 39:10-12

Potiphar believed his wife's wrongful allegation against Joseph; he threw him into prison. However, Joseph was fortunate to meet a fellow prisoner who introduced him to the King, and from there, he became the governor of the entire land of Egypt managing the whole household of King Pharoah and the resources of Egypt. From the story, we glean a wisdom nugget that God will work everything out for the good of his people.

> **"And we know [with great confidence] that God [who is deeply concerned about us] causes all things to work together [as a plan] for good for those who love God, to those who are called according to His plan *and* purpose."**
>
> ROMANS 8:28

Christians should not be yoked with unbelievers. Being unequally yoked means living by the principles of people of different beliefs and mindsets. The Bible warns against friendship with the world because one will drag the other in their direction of thoughts. Jesus warned of the danger of associations with unholy friendships or evil associations.

> **"Do not team up with those who are unbelievers. How can righteousness be a partner with wickedness? How can light live with darkness?"**
>
> 2 CORINTHIANS 6:14

Whenever a person sits with the wicked, there is a temptation to do wrong by copying their bad behaviours. This is due to peer pressure because bad people usually pressurise and intimidate innocent people into doing wrong. They cheer them on with encouraging words and approvals.

The Bible breaks the path of life into two paths, the good and the evil path. People can choose the path to follow, wickedness or righteousness, good or bad, God or idols (Deuteronomy 28). Each path has either a reward or punishment. Jesus referred to the righteous path as narrow and difficult to follow whereas the path to evil is wide, but the end is destruction.

> **"You can enter God's Kingdom only through the narrow gate. The highway to hell is broad, and its gate is wide for the many**

who choose that way. But the gateway to life is very narrow and the road is difficult, and only a few ever find it."

MATTHEW 7:13-14

The Book of Deuteronomy Chapter 28 gives a list of the blessings and curses that follows each path. The Book of Psalms chapter 1 gives a similar list of rewards for right living and the consequences for bad behaviour.

The Two Paths - Blessings and Curses

"Blessed is the man who does not walk in the counsel of the wicked or set foot on the path of sinners or sit in the seat of mockers. But his delight is in the Law of the LORD, and on His law, he meditates day and night. He is like a tree planted by streams of water, yielding its fruit in season, whose leaf does not wither, and who prospers in all he does. Not so the wicked! For they are like chaff driven off by the wind. Therefore, the wicked will not stand in the judgment, nor sinners in the assembly of the righteous. For the LORD guards the path of the righteous, but the way of the wicked will perish."

PSALM 1:1-6

PRAYER

We thank you, Lord, for the wisdom to live a righteous life. We pray for the grace to follow the path of righteousness in Jesus' name. Amen.

CHAPTER 4

Do not be Complacent or Careless

> *"For simpletons turn away from me—to death.
> Fools are destroyed by their complacency."*
>
> PROVERBS 1:32

The wisdom nugget is not to be too complacent but to be vigilant and not too satisfied because there is the danger of falling into a comfort zone where failure and destruction are bound to happen. This is like the story of the boiling frog, if left in boiling water, a frog will jump out to safety, but if placed in warm tepid water and slowly brought to the boil, it will not perceive the danger, the frog will boil to death.

The lesson is not to be complacent, negligent, or careless but to live life passionately, and stay vigilant. Spiritual, physical, and mental lukewarmness, carelessness and complacency will not let the Believer achieve a successful life. Complacency is a feeling of smugness when one has excessive self-satisfaction. It is lukewarmness, when one becomes negligent and careless, not paying attention to life or God.

The Book of Revelations Chapter 3:14-17 described the Laodicea church, they became careless in their spirituality, thereby becoming passionless.

God condemned the Believers in the Laodicea church, saying, he will vomit them out of his mouth. God loves enthusiastic people, with him there are no in-between Believers, you are either cold or hot!

Christians should make a firm choice to either serve and love God passionately or not at all, you are either on fire or dead to God! God hates those who compromise Christianity. Because those who are not fully committed to their faith, tend to love things of the world, they can backslide to join sinners in their ways. Similarly, physically, or mentally doing life half-heartedly or carelessly with no specific goals, aims or aspirations will lead to failure.

God desires his people to have an excellent spirit and not be complacent in their Christianity, so they do not fall into a routine of 'I don't care attitude,' thereby doing life in a mediocre way. Believers should live passionately, serving, and loving God wholeheartedly, drawing inspiration from the example of Jesus Christ.

Christians should live a holy life, by regularly eliminating sinful behaviour and conducting self-examination. Believers should be on fire for God, never wavering but loving him passionately. Proverbs 1:32 instructs Christians to be fervent in their faith, this applies to every Believer.

God wants his people to have a passion for Christ and to stay alert because as Apostle Peter wrote in the Book of Peter, the adversary, the Devil is always looking for whom to lead astray and cause to sin or stumble in their journey of life as Christians. So, to do life extraordinarily, Christians should be on alert, and watch and pray.

> **"Stay alert! Watch out for your great enemy, the devil. He prowls around like a roaring lion, looking for someone to devour."**
>
> 1 PETER 5:8

> **"Keep watch and pray, so that you will not give in to temptation. For the spirit is willing, but the body is weak!"**
>
> MATTHEW 26:41

PRAYER

Our Father in heaven, we pray for the courage to live life wisely, and passionately, being on fire for Christ with strength for a successful living. We ask for the power to daily watch how we live so as not to become lukewarm and careless in our actions and behaviours, in Jesus' name. Amen.

CHAPTER 5

Make Wisdom and Insight your Priority

> "Tune your ears to wisdom and concentrate on understanding. Cry out for insight and ask for understanding."
>
> PROVERBS 2:2-3

Wisdom is the quality of having experience, knowledge, and a good judgement for making sensible decisions essential for a good life. Insight, on the other hand, is having inside knowledge, a deep understanding of something, intuition, or discernment. The wisdom nugget is therefore to seek understanding and consider insight important because it is the bedrock of a successful life; by wisdom people build a beautiful life and home.

> "Through [skilful and godly] wisdom a house [a life, a home, a family] is built, and by understanding it is established [on a sound and good foundation], and by knowledge its rooms are filled with all precious and pleasant riches."
>
> PROVERBS 24:3-4

There are benefits attached to acquiring wisdom. Wisdom is useful for living a great lifestyle. A person who pursues wisdom gets the privilege of knowing God and discovering his good promises. Making wisdom a priority, therefore, means one gets the tools and instructions that are of utmost importance for success.

"Getting wisdom is the wisest thing you can do! And whatever else you do, develop good judgment."

PROVERBS 4:7

PRAYER

Father, we give you thanks, we pray for the wisdom and insight to succeed in Jesus' name. Amen.

CHAPTER 6

Trust God! Do not Assume You Know It All

> *"Trust God from the bottom of your heart; do not try to figure out everything on your own. Listen for God's voice in everything you do, everywhere you go; he is the one who will keep you on track. Do not assume that you know it all."*
>
> PROVERBS 3:5-6

The wisdom nugget is to trust God and never to assume one knows everything, thereby leaning on own understanding and ways of doing things alone. The scripture encourages Believers to seek God in prayer and to listen to his instructions in the Bible to discover hidden truths essential for daily living.

There are rewards of protection, direction, guidance, and divine health for those who obey God's commandments. The Bible promises blessings to those who trust God's counsel over their own thinking and those who shun evil and submit their will to God.

> "In all your ways know *and* acknowledge *and* recognize Him, and He will make your paths straight *and* smooth [removing obstacles that block your way]."
>
> PROVERBS 3:6

The wisest guideline for Believers in this scripture is to completely trust God for daily wisdom and guidance. The Bible promises God will make those who trust him travel on a straight path. The question to ask is, what is a straight path? It is necessary to understand God's promises because a better understanding of the benefits of God's commandments, makes them attractive to obey.

A straight path means the right way of living or doing things. Believers have a straight path to walk upon, meaning, they will walk upon level plain ground which gives them the benefit of doing life comfortably and peacefully, arriving at their expected end in life as prosperous people.

A straight path is like a red carpet rolled for celebrities; it offers Believers direction. God giving the Believer a straight path means he gives vision and direction. Trusting God, therefore, gives the people of God a red carpet signalled path for a godly and successful life.

> "Whether you turn to the right or the left, your ears will hear a voice behind you, saying, "This is the way; walk in it."
>
> ISAIAH 30:21

> "The LORD is good and does what is right; he shows the proper path to those who go astray. He leads the humble in doing right, teaching them his way."
>
> PSALM 25:8-9

Those who disobey the word of God and trust in themselves alone end in misery and self-destruction. The Bible says woe to those who are wise in their own sight (Isaiah 5:21). So, to avoid the destruction of body, soul and spirit, Christians should not live on their own terms alone, they should not become a know-it-all kind of person who fails to seek godly counsel.

Workplaces have teamwork as part of their strategy for success because when people work together, they rub minds and share wisdom which gives greater results than when just one person works on a project. Believers should, therefore, humble themselves and seek the knowledge and wisdom of God whilst surrounding themselves with wise counsellors. They should not assume they know everything, nor be deluded to think they are wiser than God or everyone else.

> **"Get all the advice and instruction you can, so you will be wise the rest of your life."**
>
> PROVERBS 19:20

> **"Stop deceiving yourselves. If you think you are wise by this world's standards, you need to become a fool to be truly wise."**
>
> 1 CORINTHIANS 3:18

PRAYER

O Lord, we pray to trust you as the source of our wisdom, we ask for the grace not to rely upon ourselves alone in Jesus' name. Amen.

CHAPTER 7

The Power of Love

> *"Let love and faithfulness never leave you; bind them around your neck, write them on the tablet of your heart."*
>
> PROVERBS 3:3

The wisdom nugget is to encourage Believers not to lose focus of God's commandment which is to love God wholeheartedly and to love their fellow human beings as they love themselves. The Bible instructs the people of God to love because it is the greatest commandment of God and love completes the law of Moses, the ten commandments. Love conquers sin and helps Christians fulfil the law of righteousness because when one loves, they will not harm others or sin against God.

> "Hear, O Israel: The Lord our God, the Lord *is* one! You shall love the Lord your God with all your heart, with all your soul, and with all your strength."
>
> DEUTERONOMY 6:4-5

"Teacher, which is the greatest commandment in the Law? Jesus replied: "Love the Lord your God with all your heart and with all your soul and with all your mind."

MATTHEW 22:36-37

The message of Jesus in the preceding scripture is to keep the law of love and be faithful to God. The question then is what is love? Apostle Paul gave a good description of the meaning of love in his letter to the Corinthians.

The Excellence of Love

"**Love endures with patience** *and* **serenity, love is kind** *and* **thoughtful, and is not jealous** *or* **envious; love does not brag and is not proud** *or* **arrogant. It is not rude; it is not self-seeking; it is not provoked [nor overly sensitive and easily angered]; it does not take into account a wrong** *endured.* **It does not rejoice at injustice but rejoices with the truth [when right and truth prevail]. Love bears all things [regardless of what comes], believes all things [looking for the best in each one], hopes all things [remaining steadfast during difficult times], endures all things [without weakening]. Love never fails [it never fades nor ends]. But as for prophecies, they will pass away; as for tongues, they will cease; as for the gift of special knowledge, it will pass away."**

1 CORINTHIANS 13:4-8

The next question is why must we practise love? Apart from love being the core message of Jesus Christ and the summary of the law of Moses, walking in love has several benefits. The benefit of love is a good reputation because love upholds a good character and help Believers do good. Love is the fruit of the Holy Spirit, it accompanies other virtues such as patience, joy, mercy, faithfulness, and goodness with which Believers can earn the wisdom to live a good and successful life. With love Christians can show compassion, be charitable and forgiving. The Bible says love covers a multitude of sins, so love is a useful tool to help Believers forgive those who offend them as demanded by God.

When one loves, there is the reward of favour from God and man. Those who show lovingkindness to people receive breakthroughs because favour opens the doors of opportunities for them. Love is the lubricant by which relationships thrive, hence Love helps Christians live a peaceful life. The Bible says love never fails and it is the answer to all issues of life. It is the greatest of all virtues!

> **"And now there remain faith [abiding trust in God and His promises], hope [confident expectation of eternal salvation], love [unselfish love for others growing out of God's love for me], these three [the choicest graces]; but the greatest of these is love."**
>
> 1 CORINTHIANS 13:13

God is a Faithful God, therefore, those who love him receive his unfailing love; his steadfast love is new every morning. And those who love people receive favour and the acceptance of people, with the reward of progress and blessing.

> **"The faithful love of the LORD never ends! His mercies never cease."**
>
> LAMENTATION 3:22

PRAYER

Father, we pray for the strength to love you wholeheartedly and grace to love our fellow human beings. We ask that you show us your unfailing love in Jesus' name. Amen.

CHAPTER 8

Honour God with Everything you Own

> "Honour the LORD with your wealth and with the best part of everything you produce."
>
> PROVERBS 3:9

The wisdom nugget is to make the fruits of your labour available for God's use. Honouring God means worshipping God with one's substance. It means showing generosity towards God's earthly agenda, using one's wealth and riches to support the kingdom of God. This can be achieved through monetary donations to churches and charities according to one's judgement.

The Book of Proverbs did not mention tithes (giving 10% of one's income to churches) but it encourages the donation of the first fruits of one's wealth, giving the best portion of one's increase, not the leftovers. Honouring God is, therefore, an exhortation to self-sacrificing devotion using personal possession for God's service.

> "Take some of the first fruits of all that you produce from the soil of the land the LORD your God is giving you and put them

in a basket. Then go to the place the LORD your God will choose as a dwelling for his name."

DEUTERONOMY 26:2

There is a reward for generosity to God, though he cannot partake in whatever Believers give, he blesses the giver with an overflow.

"Then he will fill your barns with grain, and your vats will overflow with good wine."

PROVERBS 3:10

There are also consequences to dishonouring God with gifts. The Book of Acts Chapter 5 gives an account of a couple, Ananias and Sapphira. Ananias sold a piece of property and kept part of the proceeds for himself with his wife's full knowledge. He brought only a part of the revenue to the apostles. Both husband and wife lied about the price, they claimed they gave everything, so, they dropped dead. They died as punishment for trying to deceive God the Holy Spirit with false generosity.

The lesson to Believers whenever giving for gospel work is to give generously with sincerity and fear of God. There is no minimum or maximum amount as per giving, so, giving should not be out of religiosity or ego but out of love and generosity of heart. Peter emphasised this point to Ananias before he fell dead.

"Then Peter said, "Ananias, why have you let Satan fill your heart? You lied to the Holy Spirit, and you kept some of the money for yourself. The property was yours to sell or not sell, as you wished. And after selling it, the money was also yours to give away. How could you do a thing like this? You were not lying to us but to God!"

ACTS 5:3-4

The important lesson to take away from the unfortunate story of Ananias and Sapphira is the understanding that giving belongs to God.

Even though God is not the primary receiver of gifts, his priests are his representatives on earth, so technically the gifts belong to him to be administered according to his will.

Therefore, giving is a part of Believers' worship of God. It is the Christian's financial duty and responsibility to maintain the things of God on earth which requires money and resources. Giving is therefore another way of Believers going an extra mile to love God with their possession, it proves Christians' commitment to kingdom matters and heaven's agenda on earth.

The Bible recommends Believers should give cheerfully any amount that God lays on their minds. God will reward generosity, whether small or great with abundance. Therefore, giving should be by one's heart's desire with complete honesty and sincerity making sure it is one's best offering before God.

> "Remember this—a farmer who plants only a few seeds will get a small crop. But the one who plants generously will get a generous crop. You must each decide in your heart how much to give. And do not give reluctantly or in response to pressure. "For God loves a person who gives cheerfully."
>
> 2 CORINTHIANS 9:6-7

Jesus taught of the significance of giving the best of one's substance in the story of the widow's mite. He noticed the widow casting her offering, giving just one mite whilst all others gave a little out of their abundance. The widow gave little but that was everything she had, so Jesus accounted her gift as the greatest offering of the day because the poor woman gave her all to God.

The Widow's Gift

"And He looked up and saw the rich putting their gifts into the treasury. And He saw a poor widow putting in two small copper coins. And He said, "Truly I say to you, this poor widow put in more than all *of them;* for they all out of their surplus put into the offering; but she out of her poverty put in all that she had to live on."

LUKE 21:1-4

There are examples of those who give generously in the Bible and God rose to the challenge and gave them great blessings. Solomon sacrificed one thousand burnt offerings to God and God showed up to bless him with the gift of wisdom and extraordinary wealth such that no other King of his time ever had.

> "Solomon went up to the bronze altar before the LORD in the tent of meeting and offered a thousand burnt offerings on it. That night God appeared to Solomon and said to him, "Ask for whatever you want me to give you."

2 CHRONICLES 1:6-7

> "I will certainly give you the wisdom and knowledge you requested. But I will also give you wealth, riches, and fame such as no other king has had before you or will ever have in the future!"

2 CHRONICLES 1:12

Giving to God's agenda is like giving back to him because everything belongs to him in the first instance. He is the one that teaches our hands to gain wealth, granting his people favour, strength and wisdom to prosper. God says every animal and the cattle on a thousand hills, are his (Psalm 50:10). He gives wealth to whoever he desires.

> "Thus says the LORD, your Redeemer, the Holy One of Israel: I *am* the LORD your God, who teaches you to profit, who leads you by the way you should go."

ISAIAH 48:17

Honouring God with our love and wealth is a way of obeying God's command not to forget him, and to show appreciation to him as the source of our provisions. God is our source, so, therefore, Believers must freely give back and be charitable to kingdom work, giving freely to churches founded on God's truth.

> **"You may say to yourself, "My power and the strength of my hands have produced this wealth for me. But remember the LORD your God, for it is he who gives you the ability to produce wealth, and so confirms his covenant, which he swore to your ancestors, as it is today."**
>
> DEUTERONOMY 8:17-18

Generosity may not come naturally to certain people because people have various levels of faith. The Holy Spirit bestows the gift of generosity upon certain people. Generosity is, therefore, part of the nine Fruit of the Holy Spirit, it is a spiritual gift. Those with this spiritual gift, give willingly and cheerfully, without struggle, whilst those without the gift of generosity, are usually reluctant to give because they find the act of giving difficult to do.

Regardless of whether one has the exceptional gift of generosity, the Bible recommends every Christian needs to endeavour to give out of their earnings. The measure of giving is love with the belief that whatever a person sows, he will reap with an overflow. One can conclude that giving is a form of investment that yields physical reward.

> **"Give, and you will receive. Your gift will return to you in full pressed down, shaken together to make room for more, running over, and poured into your lap. The amount you give will determine the amount you get back."**
>
> LUKE 6:38

Jesus taught gifts are a spiritual investment, a way by which Believers can store up their money in heaven where moth cannot destroy the returns on their investment. Honouring God with one's possession is a form of surrender; Believers acknowledge God as the source of their finances. The knowledge helps put money in perceptive and avoid the temptations of greed and lust for money and worldly materials. The awareness that money and all things come from God the Father because he alone has the power to give wealth, will relieve the Believer of financial anxieties.

Giving curbs human's greedy nature and helps Believers trust God for their daily needs. Apostle Paul says to the Philippians not to be anxious about their daily needs but to pray and thank God for them (Philippians 4:6-7). Jesus taught where one stores money, is where one's mind will be, so giving to God's kingdom means one will think of God's kingdom more than the world and the deceitfulness of riches.

Jesus Teaching on Money and Possession

"Do not store up for yourselves treasures on earth, where moths and vermin destroy, and where thieves break in and steal. But store up for yourselves treasures in heaven, where moths and vermin do not destroy, and where thieves do not break in and steal. For where your treasure is, there your heart will be also."

MATTHEW 6:19-21

PRAYER

Dear Lord, we pray for the grace to be generous towards kingdom work. Grant us a generous heart for your kingdom's advancement in Jesus' name. Amen.

CHAPTER 9

The Discipline of God

> "My child, don't reject the LORD's discipline, and don't be upset when he corrects you."
>
> PROVERBS 3:11

The wisdom nugget of this scripture is to accept correction without complaints. However, this presents a challenge to people because no one likes to be disciplined. The question, therefore, is why does God discipline his people? To effectively answer the question, we must first understand what discipline is.

Discipline is the practice of training people to obey rules using a reward and punishment approach to correct disobedience. So, discipline is a straightforward way to correct and guide people to the right path in life. The word of God affirms the fact that discipline is an act of love. The Bible says God disciplines those whom he loves (Proverbs 3:12).

Therefore, discipline is a blessing of God because it helps Christians mature into right-living adults who become capable members of society.

> "Those I love, I rebuke and discipline. Therefore, be earnest and repent."
>
> REVELATIONS 3:19

"So know in your heart that just as a man disciplines his son, so the LORD your God disciplines you."

DEUTERONOMY 8:5

"Blessed is the man You discipline, O LORD, and teach from Your law."

PSALM 94:12

"Blessed is the one whom God corrects; so, do not despise the discipline of the Almighty."

JOB 5:17

"And have you completely forgotten this word of encouragement that addresses you as a father addresses his son? It says, "My son, do not make light of the Lord's discipline, and do not lose heart when he rebukes you, because the Lord disciplines the one he loves, and he chastens everyone he accepts as his son."

HEBREWS 12:5-6

King David shows Christians the humble way to receive God's correction and discipline in the Book of 2 Samuel 12. God sent prophet Nathan to correct him over his adulterous relationship with Bathsheba which led to the murder of her husband, Uriah. David repented with a contrite heart so, God forgave his sin. King David wrote a psalm expressing deep remorse for his sins. In his psalm, he asked God for forgiveness, a renewed spirit and a second chance (Psalm 51).

"To the Chief Musician. A Psalm of David; when Nathan the prophet came to him after he had sinned with Bathsheba. Have mercy on me, O God, according to Your lovingkindness; According to the greatness of Your compassion blot out my transgressions."

PSALM 51:1

PRAYER

Our Father in heaven, we thank you for correcting those whom you love. We pray for the grace to value godly discipline in Jesus' name. Amen.

CHAPTER 10

Wisdom is Better than Money

> *"For wisdom is more profitable than silver, and her wages are better than gold."*
>
> PROVERBS 3:14

The wisdom nugget is wisdom is more important than money, so, it is essential to first acquire wisdom then money will naturally follow. It is more beneficial to acquire wisdom and insight than money because money is just an added benefit to wisdom. One acquires money and wealth by wisdom, and without wisdom, money will disappear due to mismanagement. With wisdom, a person can earn, grow, and multiply money through carefully selected investments.

The scripture does not disregard the fact that money is important because the Bible states money answers all things (Ecclesiastes 10:19). King Solomon told the story of a wise old man who helped a city win a war with his wisdom, but he was forgotten because he was a poor man. So, money is a great tool to have for influence and a wealthy living.

> "A poor, wise man knew how to save the town, and so it was rescued. But afterwards, no one thought to thank him."
>
> ECCLESIASTES 9:15

Solomon knows from experience and insight that wisdom is the greatest gift of God. When asked to ask for anything from God, he asked for wisdom and the gift of discerning of Spirit to rule and judge his nation to become a great leader. Choosing what is of utmost importance got him everything, wisdom, money, and influence (1 Kings 3).

PRAYER

O Lord, the giver of wisdom, we ask for wisdom and wealth in Jesus' name. Amen.

CHAPTER 11

Wisdom and Eternal Life

> "Wisdom is a tree of life to those who embrace her; happy are those who hold her tightly."
>
> PROVERBS 3:18

The wisdom nugget is to seek wisdom for the reward of eternity after a long and vibrant life. Tree of life refers to eternal life and the wellbeing enjoyed in the fullness of life offered by Jesus' redemptive work. Those who find wisdom, find the fear of God, therefore, get Jesus Christ and obtain eternal life which is the tree of life.

It is by wisdom that we understand the word of God and acknowledge the Son of God as the Messiah sent to save the world and give life abundantly (John 3:16 and John 10:10). Those who honour God, live a peaceful and healthy life. It is by wisdom that one learns to increase in years and live a long and healthy life. And it is by wisdom, that the Believers know the truth of the gospel and receive the salvation of their souls.

As previously discussed in the introduction to this book, anyone who lacks wisdom can ask God in prayer for it, the same way King Solomon asked God, his prayer was answered with wisdom and wealth. The one who receives wisdom lives a happy life and the Bible calls such a person happy and blessed (Proverbs 3:13).

Wisdom helps Christians understand the fact that they are mere mortals with limitations who need God to live successfully here on earth and his guidance to heaven for eternity with him. Wisdom opens the heart of human beings to fear and acknowledge God Almighty as the creator and saviour of humanity.

> **"LORD, remind me how brief my time on earth will be. Remind me that my days are numbered, how fleeting my life is."**
>
> PSALM 39:4

> **"Teach us to realize the brevity of life, so that we may grow in wisdom."**
>
> PSALM 90:12

PRAYER

Lord, teach us to number our days, so we may present a heart of wisdom. Grant us eternal life through your son Jesus the Messiah, in Jesus' name. Amen.

CHAPTER 12

Help Those Who Deserve a Helping Hand

> "Do not withhold good from those who deserve it when it's in your power to help them."
>
> PROVERBS 3:27

The wisdom nugget in this scripture is to help those who deserve help. Help is a gift of the Holy Spirit which means helping others come naturally to those with the gift. However, every Christian should help other people especially those of the household of God. One may not be able to help everyone, but God expects his people to do whatever is within their power and ability to help their fellow human beings in need.

The Bible teaches Christians to be kind-hearted and compassionate towards their fellow men particularly those of the family of God.

> "Therefore, as we have an opportunity, let us do good to all people, especially to those who belong to the family of believers."
>
> GALATIANS 6:10

The Message Bible Version of Proverbs 3:27 states never to walk away from someone who deserves help because the Believer's hand is the hand of God for the needy. Verse 28 further explains that Christians should not tell their neighbour: "Maybe some other time or try me tomorrow when the money is right in there in their pocket". The wisdom of this Bible Nugget is simply to help whenever one can.

Helping is a charitable act and it is an excellent way to live a godly life, according to Galatians 6:10. Believers should help fellow human beings when they have the power to do so even when they do not deserve it. The story of Joseph and his brothers is a good illustration of when family members have done harm and expected to reap evil but received mercy and help instead of what they deserve.

In the Book of Genesis chapter 42, the sons of Jacob sold off their brother Joseph as a slave, but he ended up in Egypt and his wisdom opened doors of opportunity and leadership for him at the palace, so, he became the governor who managed the household of King Pharoah and all the resources of Egypt at the time of famine.

His brothers came to Egypt to buy food and discovered Joseph was in charge. Joseph helped them by settling them in Egypt to avoid the famine. So, rather than retaliate by withholding food from them he gave them food and helped them survive.

Help, therefore, is a gift of God that Believers demonstrate by the grace of God. Whilst Christians should help others, they should exercise caution, conduct due diligence, apply wisdom, and never help at their own's expense because sometimes wicked people use Christian kindness to their advantage.

There are circumstances when Christians think they must act, though it is not within their power and ability to help, or the person does not deserve their help. One must, therefore, apply wisdom, so as not to overstretch or give what one cannot afford or fall victim to frauds, to those who just want to defraud or abuse one's kindness.

Kindness, must, therefore, be within the will of God because sometimes, kindness out of God's will is foolishness, not faith. Christians should always seek God in prayer before offering helping hands, to avoid the devil's deception which can take them out of God's will.

A notable example is an encounter between Jesus and the Devil, the devil's temptations seemed good and scriptural, but they were distractions to tempt him to sin against God and surrender his sonship to the devil (Matthew 4:1-11). So, doing good and offering a helping hand, requires wisdom and submission. It should not be an ego-driven act or a show of pretentious goodness.

PRAYER

Father, we thank you for your grace to be compassionate to others, we ask for the wisdom and insight to discern those who deserve our help in Jesus' name. Amen

CHAPTER 13
Maintain a Pure Heart

> *"Guard your heart above all else, for it determines the course of your life."*
>
> PROVERBS 4:23

The wisdom nugget is to maintain a pure heart! The Bible says to guard one's heart diligently because the heart is vital for living righteously. It is the engine of the human body, and it is from the heart, that people operate their lives, hence, the need to guard and pay attention to its use. An essential question to ask, therefore, is how does one guard the heart?

First, there is a need to define the heart and there are two definitions. The heart is the muscular organ that pumps blood through the circulatory system in human beings or animals. It is the core centre or the innermost part of human beings, the soul that powers the spirit and emotion of a person.

The heart has openings into the world through the ears, nose, eyes, mouth, tongue, hands, and feet. The openings create the sense of touch, hearing, taste, smell, sight, and movement. Human beings communicate with the world through these senses. Christians are therefore, advised to pay attention to their heart because the heart can influence their behaviour and character.

The heart is a storage system like a computer storage system, it remembers only written information. The brain collects data from the heart which it processes and sends to the senses which spill out via the mouth and influences the action of a person.

Jesus taught of the importance of maintaining a pure heart because the heart determines human behaviour, speeches, and actions. The Bible says a good person will speak good words, behave righteously, and live a godly and peaceful life, whereas a bad or evil person will blaspheme and live a destructive life.

> **"A good man brings good things out of the good stored up in his heart, and an evil man brings evil things out of the evil stored up in his heart. For the mouth speaks what the heart is full of."**
>
> LUKE 6:45

> **"For from the heart come evil thoughts, murder, adultery, all sexual immorality, theft, lying, and slander."**
>
> MATTHEW 15:19

God saw the intention of the heart of humans that he created and almost regretted creating such evil-minded people.

> **"The LORD observed the extent of human wickedness on the earth, and he saw that everything they thought or imagined was consistently evil."**
>
> GENESIS 6:5

The Bible says the heart of man is treacherously wicked and deceitful above all things, who can know it except the Spirit of God (Jeremiah 17:9). So, paying attention, and being watchful of oneself daily as one does life, is the best way to capture every thought, to prevent evil behaviour. Therefore, Believers should feed their hearts with the word of God, and meditate daily, on scriptures to live righteously.

The Bible emphasises the importance of training the heart and shutting out evil because it is essential for a successful living. In addition to meditating on the word of God, shutting the senses which are direct gateways to the heart, from evil, is necessary, to prevent the heart from becoming evil or corrupt.

According to Proverbs 23:7, as a man thinks in his heart, he becomes, meaning the thoughts of human beings will determine the course and trajectory of their lives. Apostle Paul taught the Philippians to focus on pure thoughts to enjoy a pure life because thoughts attract whatever the heart thinks about according to the law of attraction.

> "And now, dear brothers and sisters, one final thing. Fix your thoughts on what is true, honourable, right, pure, lovely, and admirable. Think about things that are excellent and worthy of praise."
>
> PHILIPPIANS 4:8

When a Believer lives in a manner that carefully monitors their thinking, their actions will be good and pleasing to God.

> "Dear friends, I urge you, as foreigners and exiles, to abstain from sinful desires, which wage war against your soul. Live such good lives among the pagans that, though they accuse you of doing wrong, they may see your good deeds and glorify God on the day he visits us."
>
> 1 PETER 2:11-12

PRAYER

Grant us a pure heart O Lord! Teach us how to guard our hearts with diligence, so our behaviours will be pleasing to you in Jesus' name, we pray. Amen.

CHAPTER 14

Honest and Pure Communication

> *"Avoid all perverse talk; stay away from corrupt speech."*
>
> PROVERBS 4:24

The wisdom nugget is to pay attention to the mouth and keep it pure and honest. As the heart is vital to living righteously, the mouth is equally essential to upright living. The Bible says out of the abundance of the heart the mouth speaks (Matthew 12:34) because thought will develop into overwhelming feelings and emotions that will eventually express themselves in speech or behaviour.

The heart and the mouth relate to each other. Both are vital to godly living. God wants his people to avoid perverse talk and bad communication. Therefore, the wisdom is for Christians to develop honest communications. Believers should learn to tame their tongue to speak good and not perverse talk. That will only be possible by filling the heart with good thoughts.

One may ask, what does perverse talk mean? It is simply a deceitful talk, that is, when a person lies or misleads people. This is contrary to how God wants his children to do life. God is God of Truth; he is honest, and the Bible declares there is no falsehood in him. God wants Believers to live a truthful and upright life.

The Psalmist (writer of the Book of Psalms) wrote a guide on how to maintain a pure mouth in the Book of Psalm chapter 1. The Psalmist gives tips on how to avoid perverse and deceitful talk, and the key secret is to stay away from bad associations because their communications will corrupt good people.

However, in addition to staying clear of perverted people whose thoughts and speeches are unreasonable or unacceptable, Believers should watch their hearts as well. As already discussed in the previous chapter, the heart is the source of all speeches. Therefore, Apostle Paul asked the Philippians to stay focused on their thoughts to maintain a pure heart.

Jesus spoke to the people to guard their hearts because out of it comes the words and actions of human beings. He said, when a tree is good, the fruit will also be good. So, therefore if a person wants to have good and clean communication, there is a need to take care of the heart which is the source from which speeches spring forth.

> "You brood of snakes! How could evil men like you speak what is good and right? For whatever is in your heart determines what you say."
>
> MATTHEW 12:34

The Psalmist wrote clean speeches come from clean lips, he, therefore, asked God in prayer for a spiritual guard on his lips to maintain clean lips. Christians can, therefore, request clean lips from God in prayer.

> "Take control of what I say, O LORD, and guard my lips."
>
> PSALM 141:3

Righteous living requires clean the lips and a pure mouth which in turn requires a pure heart. The good news is that both prayer and training of the heart and lips will generate a great life for the Believer. Training helps the heart, feeding it with the word of God daily helps it become perfect. Proverbs 10:32 says the lips of the righteous know what is fitting but that of the wicked is perverse.

Believers must pay conscious attention to the use of their mouths, particularly in daily speeches. James compared the training of the mouth to that of a horse which is difficult to control. But he emphasised the need to control the tongue.

> **"Those who consider themselves religious and yet do not keep a tight rein on their tongues deceive themselves, and their religion is worthless."**
>
> JAMES 1:26

James' Teaching About the Tongue

"Not many of you should become teachers, my fellow believers because you know that we who teach will be judged more strictly. We all stumble in many ways. Anyone who is never at fault in what they say is perfect, able to keep their whole body in check. When we put bits into the mouths of horses to make them obey us, we can turn the whole animal. Or take ships as an example. Although they are so large and are driven by strong winds, they are steered by a very small rudder wherever the pilot wants to go. Likewise, the tongue is a small part of the body, but it makes great boasts. Consider what a great forest is set on fire by a small spark. The tongue also is a fire, a world of evil among the parts of the body. It corrupts the whole body, sets the whole course of one's life on fire, and is itself set on fire by hell. All kinds of animals, birds, reptiles, and sea creatures are being tamed and have been tamed by mankind, but no human being can tame the tongue. It is a restless evil, full of deadly poison. With the tongue, we praise our Lord and Father, and with it, we curse human beings, who have been made in God's likeness. Out of the same mouth come praise and cursing. My brothers and sisters, this should not be. Can both fresh water and saltwater flow from the same spring? My brothers and sisters, can a fig tree bear olive, or a grapevine bear fig? Neither can a salt spring produce fresh water."

JAMES 3:1-12

Guarding the mouth comes with a reward, the Bible declares anyone who guards his mouth, protects his life, but one who opens his lips recklessly invites his ruin (Proverbs 21:23). The consequences of not paying attention to the mouth are failure, death, and destruction. To enjoy a peaceful life, one should guard the mouth and earn the reward of long and peaceful life.

James gives Believers a tip on how to achieve a truthful mouth. He advised Christians to be slow to speak and quick to hear. That way, one will get sufficient time to process their thought before expressing them through speeches.

> "Understand this, my dear brothers and sisters: You must all be quick to listen, slow to speak, and slow to get angry."

JAMES 1:19

The wisdom of James' teaching is to allow time to process information thoroughly before using such information in one's speeches. Christians should pay attention to hearing because it relates to speaking and doing. The Psalmist writes that he will watch his ways so that he will not sin with his tongue.

> "For the director of music. For Jeduthun. A psalm of David. I said, "I will watch my ways and keep my tongue from sin; I will put a muzzle on my mouth while in the presence of the wicked."

PSALM 39:1

PRAYER

Father, we pray that you set a guard over our mouths and keep watch on the door of our lips, so we may stay away from deceitful life and corrupt communication in Jesus' name. Amen.

CHAPTER 15

Focus and Moral Standard

> "Let your eyes look directly ahead [toward the path of moral courage] And let your gaze be fixed straight in front of you [toward the path of integrity]."
>
> PROVERBS 4:25

The wisdom nugget is to pay attention to the eyes which is the way by which a person maintains focus on the important moral standards of life. Christians must focus and avoid worldly temptations; they must develop the power and ability to focus on the vital matters of life. To succeed in life, one must have clarity of purpose, a vision accompanied by goals and wise planning. A solid intention to do life in a certain carefully selected manner. This requires effort and time with God and his laws.

Learning to curb the eyesight spiritually is key to how a person does life. There are distractions and sideshows in the world which can easily weigh God's people down, causing them to get distracted, tempted to do evil or live a sinful life. Evil things, tend to glitter like gold and worldly things can entice the Believer beyond their limit and cause them to stumble.

The solution is to be determined and to stay focused on God, Isaiah said to set the face like flint with a determination never to yield to sin but to fulfil the will of God. Maintaining a good focus requires the Believer to be resolute and follow the example of Jesus.

> **"Because the Sovereign LORD helps me, I will not be disgraced. Therefore, I have set my face like a stone, determined to do his will. And I know that I will not be put to shame."**
>
> ISAIAH 50:7

The word of God teaches the Believer to be rigid in their vision of life, to look straight ahead, and not to succumb to distractions which only lead people astray. It is worth noting that distractions may come in form of evil masquerading as good, so one must be aware of the devil's tactics and pay attention to the instructions of God.

The Book of Genesis Chapter 3 gave an account of the encounter between the first woman Eve and Satan. Eve was deceived into the sin of disobedience which eventually caused the spiritual death of the first man Adam. The entire universe fell into the Adamic sin because of Eve's lustful desire for the forbidden fruit which she saw and considered good for food. The Bible says people with no focus, fall into temptations and sin because of their evil desires and lustful eyes.

> **"But each one is tempted when he is dragged away, enticed *and* baited [to commit sin] by his own [worldly] desire (lust, passion)."**
>
> JAMES 1:14

God warned her husband Adam not to eat from the tree of life, but she ate it and shared it with Adam. From the experience came the curse of death and hell. But thank God, the second Adam, Jesus Christ saved humanity from their sin by paying the price and wages of sin, which is death. Jesus was of a different spirit, he focused on the job at hand and conquered Satan. He overcame the devil's temptations and proposals with the word of God.

Jesus had clarity of purpose and his desires were under control because he was submissive to the will of God the Father. The devil wanted to lead him astray with perverted vision and worldly gains, but he ignored all distractions and defeated Satan.

> "Again, the devil took him to a very high mountain and showed him all the kingdoms of the world and their splendour. "All this I will give you," he said, "if you will bow down and worship me. Jesus said to him, "Away from me, Satan! For it is written: 'Worship the Lord your God and serve him only. Then the devil left him, and angels came and attended him."
>
> MATTHEW 4:8-11

Christians in addition to determination and the application of the word of God can pray for focus. Since most sins happen because human beings cannot control their sight, believers can pray for self-control. Job's solution is to make a covenant with God and with determination and self-control fight to maintain a godly focus to avoid lust.

> "I made a covenant with my eyes not to look lustfully at a young woman."
>
> JOB 31:1

However, King David's lack of self-control and self-discipline caused him to commit adultery as mentioned previously. Christians must maintain their focus on God and follow the examples of Jesus and the instructions of God in his word, putting their faith in Christ Jesus, who is the author and perfecter of their faith.

> "Therefore, since we are surrounded by such a huge crowd of witnesses to the life of faith, let us strip off every weight that slows us down, especially the sin that so easily trips us up. And let us run with endurance the race God has set before us. We do this by keeping our eyes on Jesus, the champion who

initiates and perfects our faith. Because of the joy awaiting him, he endured the cross, disregarding its shame. Now he is seated in the place of honour beside God's throne."

HEBREWS 12:1-2

The wisdom for doing life successfully from this scripture is to keep one's gaze on Jesus, learn the word of God and apply it to life's circumstances and have godly vision and desires. Apostle Paul says he keeps his gaze on the goal and future prize.

"I press on toward the goal to win the [heavenly] prize of the upward call of God in Christ Jesus."

PHILIPPIANS 3:14

PRAYER

Dear Lord, we ask for pure eyesight, so that we behold only pure things with our eyes, to enjoy a long life free of sin. Grant us O Lord, godly heart desires, so, we do not get distracted and sin in Jesus' name. Amen.

CHAPTER 16

Flee Immorality

> "So, my friend, listen closely; do not treat my words casually. Keep your distance from such a woman; stay out of her neighbourhood. You do not want to squander your wonderful life, to waste your precious life among the hard-hearted. Why should you allow strangers to take advantage of you?"
>
> PROVERBS 5:8-11

The wisdom nugget is to flee from wayward women and immoral people, who will merely use and discard their victims. Christians should avoid adultery and fornication, by carefully selecting friendships and keeping at bay evil women or evil associations. Who would know better than King Solomon? He was a product of an adulterous relationship between his father King David and his mother Bathsheba. Furthermore, he had the experience of foreign women enticing him to worship foreign gods.

A notable example of how to deal with sexual temptation is the story of Joseph who physically fled from the grasp of his Egyptian master Potiphar's wife (Genesis 39:11-12). The Believer should physically avoid negative influence by sinners. Psalm 1 gives the advice to not sit with wicked people because they tend to persuade others to join in their wicked behaviours. So, the wisdom of this scripture, simply put, is to stay away from bad relationships. Christians should avoid friendships that introduce them to immorality or any form of sin that gets them distracted from the righteous path of life.

To do life in a holy manner and enjoy a life free of regrets in one's old age, one must flee immorality and have moral courage. The consequence of an immoral life is usually devastation because sin permits Satan, the devourer to come in and steal one's wealth, strength, ideas, visions, God's purpose, and divine direction for one's life. Therefore, the Bible warns the Believers, not to join with unbelievers because unequal yoke will cause them to stumble in their walk with God.

> **"Do not team up with those who are unbelievers. How can righteousness be a partner with wickedness? How can light live with darkness?"**
>
> 2 CORINTHIANS 6:14

> **"When I wrote to you before, I told you not to associate with people who indulge in sexual sin."**
>
> 1 CORINTHIANS 5:9

PRAYER

Father, we pray for Believers all over the world that they will stay away from immorality and evil associations. We ask for wisdom and moral courage in Jesus' name. Amen.

CHAPTER 17

Take Wise Decisions

> "He will die for lack of self-control; he will be lost because of his great foolishness."
>
> PROVERBS 5:23

The wisdom nugget is to have self-control which is a fruit of the Holy Spirit and the ability to discipline oneself. Having self-control, helps the Believer take wise decisions and righteous actions in life. The scripture warns the Believer against immorality and evil desires which can cause them to stumble into sin and fail to live wisely.

Christians must therefore learn to harness themselves, reigning in their emotions and carnality. We have learnt of the story of Eve and how her encounter with the Devil, caused the fall of humanity due to her disobedience in previous chapters. She lacked self-control and took bad decisions that made her sin, due to her lustful eyes and lack of self-discipline. The key to successful living, therefore, is to subdue oneself and guard against lustful eyes and evil desires.

Great leaders have fallen because of a lack of self-control towards what they saw, leading them to make bad decisions, unholy actions, or sin. The sin of lustful eyes does not just happen to Kings and great leaders but all of humanity. One must, therefore, avoid seeing evil to avoid doing evil, because the Believer will make bad decisions without self-discipline.

Jesus was emphatic about the eyes of people having a great ability to distract and lead them astray that he said to pluck evil eyes out spiritually. Jesus believes the eyes can cause the Believer to see worldly things and fall into temptation, so he was drastic in his teachings, challenging Believers to give up evil eyes for pure eyesight. Wrong desires generated from lustful eyesight, can make people take decisions that lead to sinful actions.

> **And if your eye causes you to sin, gouge it out and throw it away. It is better to enter eternal life with only one eye than to have two eyes and be thrown into the fire of hell."**
>
> MATTHEW 18:9

Jesus was able to overcome all forms of evil desires because he kept his focus on God the Father saying and doing only what the Father ask him to say or do. Believers can also avoid bad decisions by keeping their gaze on Jesus the author and finisher of their faith. This is having vision or focus as discussed in previous chapters; it eliminates all distractions and helps Christians make wise decisions.

PRAYER

Father, we pray for every Believer, we ask that you grant them self-control and the grace to make wise decisions in Jesus' name. Amen.

CHAPTER 18

Renegotiate Bad Deals

> "My child, if you have put up security for a friend's debt or agreed to guarantee the debt of a stranger if you have trapped yourself by your agreement and are caught by what you said, follow my advice and save yourself, for you have placed yourself at your friend's mercy. Now swallow your pride; go and beg to have your name erased."
>
> PROVERBS 6:1-3

The wisdom nugget in this scripture is a simple guideline to follow if one falls into a bad deal. To escape the monetary loss of bad judgement, one must guide against arrogance, or egoistic foolishness and humble oneself to renegotiate the deal, and where necessary beg for mercy from the other person. The Bible compares the situation with that of a deer caught in a chase by a hunter, the deer do a flight to avoid death by the hunter. Likewise, a Believer should run from unmanageable debt and find a way to escape from the responsibility of bad debt.

The Bible emphasised Believers should pay attention to such matters and not sweep them under the carpet because they will end up in greater trouble. The correct way of managing such matters is to plead with the other party and ask for release from the obligations as a matter of urgency.

"Do not put it off; do it now! Do not rest until you do."

PROVERBS 6:4

PRAYER

Father, we thank you for your word and guidelines to help us live life successfully, we ask for the grace to avoid bad deals and bad financial decisions that can ruin our lives in Jesus' name. Amen.

CHAPTER 19

Be Organised – Work Smart!

> *"Take a lesson from the ants, you, lazybones. Learn from their ways and become wise!"*
>
> **PROVERBS 6:6**

The wisdom nugget of this scripture is to avoid laziness, to work smart, and be well organised, wise, and hardworking. To observe the ways of the ants, who have no leadership, yet work as a team to gather their food, they know how to prepare their provision for all seasons. The Bible is using the analogy of the ant to teach the Believer how to do life by being diligent and wise, preparing for all seasons of life.

Seasons could be according to one's age. One ought to gather money through earning wages from work or profits from business transactions and interests from savings and investments. Believers should apply financial wisdom to spending, savings, and investments. The common-sense approach to financial freedom is to work and save part of the earnings for the future.

Investments such as a pension, interest-yielding bank savings, stocks, bonds, life, and health insurance are useful packages that can help the

Believer prepare for emergencies, retirement, and old age. The ants know when to act, they know how to discern the times, they are wonderful time managers and they know the time to sow, and the time to gather their harvest. They are well organised, hardworking, and great collaborators. They work in unity gathering their food in summer, with surplus left over for the winter season. They are cooperative with one another, understanding the importance of teamwork.

King Solomon further illustrated this wisdom nugget in the Book of Ecclesiastes teaching about the various times and seasons of life (Ecclesiastes 3:1-8). The Believer should, therefore, understand how seasons of life work and plan their lives accordingly financially.

PRAYER

Dear Lord, we thank you for your word and godly counsel, we ask that we learn from the organised way of the ant to put our lives in order financially in Jesus' name. Amen.

CHAPTER 20
Be Diligent – Work Hard!

> *"But you, lazybones, how long will you sleep? When will you wake up?"*
>
> PROVERBS 6:9

The Bible warns of the consequences of laziness caused by oversleeping, stating that whoever slacks in his work, becomes poor (Proverbs 18:9). But the diligent in their work will gain tremendous wealth. The wisdom nugget is, therefore, to work hard and avoid unnecessary sleep. Christians should have a balanced life pattern where there is time allocated to different activities of life such as sleep, work, meals, and relaxation.

The average sleep hours for human beings are between six to eight hours per day. Sleep usually happens during the night unless a person works night shift. Therefore, to succeed in life, one must have self-discipline and not oversleep. The average sleeping hours recommended is eight hours, except in occasional cases of sicknesses, when one requires additional rest to recover.

Work time is also an average of 8 hours per day. The balance of work and sleep will bring increase and prosperity to the Believer. People who work and are not lazy usually do well in life whereas the lazybones fail and live in poverty. So, the harsh but wise lesson of this scripture is to alert people to the hardships of laziness. God wants everyone who is physically and mentally able, to do their best and work in exchange for their livelihood.

There is a great reward of riches for those who work, and poverty and lack for those who waste their years in slumber and laziness. Diligence results in wealth whereas laziness tends to poverty (Proverbs 10:4). The Bible warns poverty will lead to ruin and destruction.

> **"The wealth of the rich is their fortress; the poverty of the poor is their destruction."**
>
> PROVERBS 10:15

PRAYER

Dear Lord, we thank you for the ability and the skill to work. We pray you will give Believers the grace to work at the appropriate times and seasons of life. We pray Christians will not waste their life and time by being lazy, so they can live a happy and prosperous life in Jesus' name. Amen.

CHAPTER 21

Detestable Behaviours

> "There are six things the LORD hates, seven that are detestable to him: haughty eyes, a lying tongue, hands that shed innocent blood, a heart that devises wicked schemes, feet that are quick to rush into evil, a false witness who pours out lies and a person who stirs up conflict in the community."
>
> PROVERBS 6:16-19

The Bible states the fear of the Lord is the beginning of wisdom, it is knowing the things God likes or dislikes that helps the Believer live a righteous and prosperous life in holy fear of God. The wisdom nugget in these scriptures is to know what God hates and avoid doing them. The spiritual success of Believers will lead to their general success in life.

This chapter will attempt to break down all the seven things God hates with suggestions of how to do life successfully by avoiding the seven evils. The Bible states there are six things the LORD hates, seven that are detestable to him (Proverbs 6:16-19).

The Seven Things God Hates

1. Haughty eyes
2. A lying tongue
3. Hands that shed innocent blood
4. A heart that devises wicked schemes
5. Feet that are quick to rush into evil
6. A false witness who pours out lies
7. A person who stirs up conflict in the community

Let us go through the list to understand why God hates such behaviours and why he does not tolerate them from his people.

Haughty eyes: This is an arrogant eye; it means a proud person, and the Bible states God hates pride. Proud and conceited people with self-importance and an exaggerated self-opinion are unacceptable to God.

> **"Because of the privilege and authority God has given me, I give each of you this warning: Do not think you are better than you are. Be honest in your evaluation of yourselves, measuring yourselves by the faith God has given us.**
>
> ROMANS 12:3

Looking down on other people and thinking one is better than others is a despicable act before God Almighty. Believers ought to be humble because God rewards humility and punishes pride. Humility leads to promotion whereas pride leads to destruction and ruin.

> **"The reward for humility and fear of the LORD is riches and honour and life."**
>
> PROVERBS 22:4

> **"Pride goes before destruction, and haughtiness before a fall."**
>
> PROVERBS 16:18

A lying tongue: This is a person with a perverse mouth, one who tells lies with speeches full of deceit. They are usually malicious and speak falsehood to deceive others. One of the laws given to God's people is not to lie or bear false witness against their neighbours. God instructs his people to walk in love with their fellow men, lying or giving false testimonies to harm others is not an act of love but hate.

> "Do not steal; Do not lie; Do not deceive one another."
>
> LEVITICUS 19:11

> "Do not seek revenge or bear a grudge against anyone among your people but love your neighbour as yourself. I am the LORD."
>
> LEVITICUS 19:18

The hand that sheds innocent blood: This is someone who kills people with the intent to commit murder. God forbids the shedding of innocent blood in the Old Testament Bible. In the New Testament Bible, Jesus took God's condemnation of murder further to include other acts of wickedness that cause harm to others.

> "You shall not commit murder (unjustified, deliberate homicide).
>
> EXODUS 20:13

> "You have heard that our ancestors were told, you must not murder. If you commit murder, you are subject to judgment. But I say, if you are even angry with someone, you are subject to judgment! If you call someone an idiot, you are in danger of being brought before the court. And if you curse someone, you are in danger of the fires of hell."
>
> MATTHEW 5:21-22

A heart that devices wicked schemes: This is a person that devises evil plans, their ways of doing things or handling matters is usually immoral and wrong. God calls such people evil and wicked, with their end being death and destruction. Believers must, therefore, abstain from conniving and inventing evil schemes and strategies that harm their fellow human beings.

Real-life stories show schemes devised against rivals or opponents usually fail and boomerang on the wicked person or their loved ones be it in business, politics, or general living. The Believers should align their hearts with God's commandment of love by doing good to their fellow human beings.

Furthermore, the Bible recommends, Believers should forgive and give offences up to God's avenging power. The Bible says, human beings have treacherously wicked hearts, so, Christians should, therefore, pay attention to their thoughts, ensuring their thinking, plans and actions are in line with the word of God, the Bible.

A simple test is to make sure every plan satisfies the commandment of God to love one's neighbour (other human beings). Apostle Paul gives Christians tips on how to do life with a pure heart in his letter to the Philippians.

> **"And now, dear brothers and sisters, one final thing. Fix your thoughts on what is true, honourable, right, pure, lovely, and admirable. Think about things that are excellent and worthy of praise."**
>
> PHILIPPIANS 4:8

When the human heart focuses on pure thoughts and the word of God, it will defeat the human nature that tends toward evil behaviour and wickedness. The Hymn, Trust and Obey, suggests the Believer should walk with the Lord in the light of his word, trusting and obeying him. Then, they will win in life, and live victoriously with a pure, godly, and sincere heart. Anyone who lives in this manner will be invincible, powerful, and undefeated. They will succeed in their Christian journey with God.

Feet that run to evil: This one applies to people who execute evil plans against others. Their thought is sinful, and it leads them into committing crimes and evil behaviour.

> **"Their feet run to do evil, and they rush to commit murder. They think only about sinning. Misery and destruction always follow them."**
>
> ISAIAH 59:7

> **"Their mouths are full of cursing and bitterness. They rush to commit murder. Destruction and misery always follow them."**
>
> ROMANS 3:14-16

The wisdom nugget is to guard against committing violent crimes that destroy the lives of innocent people. The secret to achieving and doing life in a crime-free manner is to read the word of God, the Bible and apply its principles to life circumstances. That is the application of the word that the Bible calls observing God's word.

> **"Your word is a lamp to guide my feet and a light for my path."**
>
> PSALM 119:105

> **"I have refused to walk on any evil path, so that I may remain obedient to your word."**
>
> PSALM 119:101

A false witness who pours out lies: This is a person who tells a falsehood, they falsify documents and give misleading evidence against innocent people, especially their opponents or rivals. Those who bear false witnesses are particularly despicable to God because they do not just tell lies to protect themselves from harm, they tell harmful lies with the aim and intent to harm others, either in exchange for monetary gain or out of fear and intimidation from other people for their selfish gain.

Their lies contribute to the condemnation of another person who may be innocent. Exodus 20:16 emphasised that Believers must not bear false witness against their neighbours.

> "You must not testify falsely against your neighbour."
>
> EXODUS 20:16

A person who stirs up conflict in the community: This is a person who instigates trouble, an inciter or provoker of other people to commit crime or evil. The Bible instructs Believers to be peacemakers because troublemakers are despicable to God (Matthew 5:9). The Book of Titus advised Believers to avoid foolish controversies and quarrels which can destabilise communities.

> "Do not get involved in foolish discussions about spiritual pedigrees or quarrels and fights about obedience to Jewish laws. These things are useless and a waste of time. If people are causing divisions among you, give a first and second warning. After that, have nothing more to do with them. For people like that have turned away from the truth, and their owns condemn them."
>
> TITUS 3:9-11

Timothy further warns Believers to avoid instigators, troublemakers and influencers that can corrupt good character.

> "Remind everyone about these things, and command them in God's presence to stop fighting over words. Such arguments are useless, and they can ruin those who hear them."
>
> 2 TIMOTHY 2:14

> "Again, I say, don't get involved in foolish, ignorant arguments that only start fights."
>
> 2 TIMOTHY 2:23

It is, therefore, paramount that the Believer should pay attention to the things God hates because they corrupt the heart. An excellent way to live free of these detestable things is to operate and do life from a clean and pure heart.

King David realised this fact when he sinned, so, he quickly repented and prayed to God for a pure heart and clean hands so he will not shed innocent blood again. Human thought determines the course of life, so, Christians should keep their heart pure and free from unholy thoughts.

> **"Create in me a clean heart, O God. Renew a loyal spirit within me."**
>
> PSALM 51:10

The Gospel is a message of hope and good news, so, there is hope for people who have committed the sins that God hates. The Bible preaches a message of hope and forgiveness which offers the opportunity to start afresh by repenting and turning away from evil behaviours. King David, repented of his sins and God forgave him.

> **"Forgive me for shedding blood, O God who saves; then I will joyfully sing of your forgiveness."**
>
> PSALM 51:14

The Bible says there is no condemnation in Christ Jesus, once a person gives their life to God, they become a new creation with every sin pardoned.

> **"Therefore, there is now no condemnation for those who are in Christ Jesus because through Christ Jesus the law of the Spirit who gives life has set you free from the law of sin and death.**

For what the law was powerless to do because it was weakened by the flesh, God did by sending his own Son in the likeness of sinful flesh to be a sin offering. And so, he condemned sin in the flesh. He did this so that the just requirement of the law would be fully satisfied for us, who no longer follow our sinful nature but instead follow the Spirit."

ROMANS 8:1-4

PRAYER

Dear Lord, we are thankful, that you teach us your way by letting us know what you consider despicable to you. We ask for the grace to live a life that is pure and pleasing to you in Jesus' name. Amen.

CHAPTER 22

A Beautiful Life for the Godly

> *"The wages of the righteous is life, but the earnings of the wicked are sin and death."*
>
> **PROVERBS 10:16**

The Bible promises a reward of exuberant life for those who live righteously. Therefore, by living an upright life, Believers will earn the reward of a happy, vibrant, and long life. The Bible teaches that righteous people will enjoy beautiful and abundant life whilst those who do wickedly will end in sin, frustration, and destruction.

> *"Tell the godly that all will be well for them. They will enjoy the rich reward they have earned!"*
>
> ISAIAH 3:10

The righteous will reap the reward of their godly actions, which are the fullness of life and happiness. God rewards good behaviour with prosperity and peace. The Bible says people reap whatever they sow, so good deeds will yield a bountiful harvest of goodness.

"Do not be misled you cannot mock the justice of God. You will always harvest what you plant. Those who live only to satisfy their sinful nature will harvest decay and death from that sinful nature. But those who live to please the Spirit will harvest everlasting life from the Spirit."

GALATIANS 6:7-8

"I will reward them with a long life and give them my salvation."

PSALM 91:16

The good news is not to give up on doing good because God will eventually reward your charitable deeds. The Bible states righteous deeds will yield a bountiful harvest of blessing.

"So, let us not get tired of doing what is good. At just the right time we will reap a harvest of blessing if we do not give up."

GALATIANS 6:9

PRAYER

Dear Lord, we thank you for your word that refreshes and encourages us, we ask for the grace to live a righteous and good life. We pray for a life that is pleasing to you, so, we can enjoy a vibrant and full life in Jesus' name. Amen.

CHAPTER 23

Lust and Adultery

> "But the man who commits adultery is an utter fool, for he destroys himself."
>
> PROVERB 6:32

Adultery is when a person in the union of marriage has voluntary sexual intercourse with a person who is not their spouse. The Bible forbids adultery because it is a sin against both soul and body. The wisdom nugget is to stay away from cheating on one's partner within the contractual relationship of marriage.

> "You must not commit adultery."
>
> EXODUS 20:14

Hebrews 13:4 teaches about marriage, stating marriage should be pure and free of deceit, with the marriage vows honoured by both parties. Trust is a crucial factor for a successful marriage, so, sexual betrayal violates the integrity of marriage. Married couples should, therefore, ensure to keep their marriage bed undefiled from sexual sins of adultery and immorality.

Apostle Paul's Teaching About Maintaining the Integrity of Marriage

> "Marriage should be honoured by all, and the marriage bed kept pure, for God will judge the adulterer and all the sexually immoral."
>
> HEBREWS 13:4

Jesus extended his teaching on adultery from physical sexual intercourse to lustful looks and unholy sexual heart desires. Wanting Believers to do better than the Pharisees in matters of God's laws and right living, he said, adultery is more than sexual interaction with another outside of the marriage union. Lustful looks and unholy feelings towards another person other than one's spouse amount to adultery. Adultery, therefore, is a matter of the heart because it begins with what the eye sees which goes into the heart and becomes fulfilled in the physical act of adultery.

Jesus Extends Adultery to Include Lust

> "You have heard the commandment that says, 'You must not commit adultery. But I say, anyone who even looks at a woman with lust has already committed adultery with her in his heart."
>
> MATTHEW 5:27-28

Therefore, the Book of Proverbs says adultery is a sin that can destroy the soul. A sin conceived in the heart corrupts the heart of a person and leads them into destructive actions of sexual sin. Sex has a way of messing with the human soul and mind, it leads to addictive behaviour and consumes a person's time and energy.

The sin of adultery prevents spiritual growth, it brings guilt, isolation, rejection, and condemnation to the soul. It debars personal progress because the cheated partner may decide to file for divorce which usually creates issues for the entire family. Divorce is expensive, and legal fees can cost financial stress if the partners cannot resolve their issues peacefully. The separation that follows creates disruption in the family which can impact any child involved negatively.

> "Run from sexual sin! No other sin so clearly affects the body as this one does. For sexual immorality is a sin against your own body."
>
> 1 CORINTHIANS 6:18

The Bible, therefore, advise the people of God to flee from adultery because it becomes a habit, and causes deceit and emotional pain. The person engaged in sinful activities of adultery usually feels ashamed and prefers to keep things secret, so they lie to keep their secrets. The solution is to abstain from sexual immorality and enjoy sex from one's partner, letting them enjoy the happiness of fidelity and loyalty in their marriage.

> "Let your fountain (wife) be blessed [with the rewards of fidelity] And rejoice in the wife of your youth."
>
> PROVERBS 5:18

Joseph provides an excellent way to deal with the temptation of adultery. When asked by his master Potiphar's wife to sleep with her, he ran from the room, physically escaping the situation (Genesis 39:11-12). King David on the other hand followed the lusting of his eyes and slept with his soldier's wife, Bathsheba, (2 Samuel 11:4), thereby, sinning against God and his commandment not to commit adultery.

The story of King David brings hope to the situation, his experience is a good illustration that whoever sins can repent and have God's forgiveness. God is a God of restoration, so, he will forgive the error of judgement of adultery for whoever repents and turn from their deceitful ways.

However, the fact that God forgives does not mean there will not be consequences for the sin. For instance, the other partner may refuse to forgive, escalating the matter to divorce, based on the legal ground of adultery. An effective way to avoid sexual immorality and adultery, is, therefore, to keep one's eyes away from evil and avoid bad associations with those who disregard holy matrimony.

PRAYER

Father, we thank you for your word and commandment that forbids adultery of the soul and body. We pray you will help Believers to keep their marital vows and marriage holy in Jesus' name. Amen.

CHAPTER 24

Mercy and Forgiveness

> *"Hatred stirs up quarrels, but love makes up for all offences."*
>
> PROVERBS 10:12

The wisdom nugget is to practise forgiveness and forgive people who offend you. The act of love, mercy and forgiveness will help Christians live life peacefully. Love fulfils all righteousness and prevents fights and hatred. The importance of loving one's fellow human beings gives Believer the ability to forgive and show mercy and compassion to people.

Love lifts Christians above offences, meanwhile, hatred makes one lose control, thereby, falling into the sin of anger and hatred which eventually lead to bitterness, violence, and fighting. Love provides Believers with the grace to walk away from strife and insults, it gives them the power to forgive and overlook minor offences.

Forgiveness results in great relationships and long life, it prevents emotional surge that sometimes shocks the nervous system into producing unhealthy hormones that cause diseases. Forgiveness is, therefore, an antidote for hormonal-induced sicknesses and diseases in human beings. A loving heart generates a happy, peaceful, and blessed life. Jesus taught his disciples to show mercy and forgiveness during prayer, so, God the Father can also forgive their sins.

The Lord's Prayer and Forgiveness

"For if you forgive others their trespasses [their reckless and wilful sins], your heavenly Father will also forgive you."

MATTHEW 6:14

Forgiveness means trusting God to compensate and avenge offences, Christians must give up their right to punish and take revenge for offences or wrongs. Apostle Peter encourages Believers to love and show kindness to others, forgiving them without complaints. And Apostle Paul preaches likewise.

"Most importantly, continue to show deep love for each other, for love covers a multitude of sins."

1 PETER 4:8

"Bearing graciously with one another, and willingly forgiving each other if one has a cause for complaint against another; just as the Lord has forgiven you, so should you forgive."

COLOSSIANS 3:13

The Bible states that love and forgiveness save people from sin and death. One who conceals an offence promotes love and ends hatred among people.

"He who covers *and* forgives an offence seeks love, but he who repeats *or* gossips about a matter separates intimate friends."

PROVERBS 17:9

"Let the [latter] one know that the one who has turned a sinner from the error of his way will save that one's soul from death and cover a multitude of sins [that is, obtain the pardon of the many sins committed by the one who has been restored]."

JAMES 5:20

PRAYER

Dear Lord, we pray for the grace to be merciful and forgiving, showing mercy and compassion to our fellow human beings in Jesus' name. Amen.

CHAPTER 25

Beware of Deception

> "Hiding hatred makes you a liar; slandering others makes you a fool."
>
> PROVERBS 10:18

The wisdom nugget is to beware of deceptive people. The Bible declares a hateful heart is the source of lying, simply put, lies flow from a hateful heart. The heart is the engine of all human actions, it is from the heart that issues of life spring forth. The Bible says a good person with a good heart will show love, speak the truth and be free of deceit. But those with a hateful heart produce the fruit of their hatred which is deceitfulness, falsehood, and malice.

The Bible says those who lie are the children of Satan because their father is a liar from the beginning. They disguise their hate with fake pleasant and flattering words. But their heart is full of deceit and hate towards their prey.

> "You are of *your* father the devil, and it is your will to practice the desires [which are characteristic] of your father. He was a murderer from the beginning and does not stand in the truth because there is no truth in him. When he lies, he speaks what is natural to him, for he is a liar and the father of lies *and* half-truths."
>
> JOHN 8:44

> "Their malice may be concealed by deception, but their wickedness will be exposed in the assembly."
>
> PROVERBS 26:26

> "People may cover their hatred with pleasant words, but they're deceiving you."
>
> PROVERBS 10:18

> "A good man brings good things out of the good stored up in his heart, and an evil man brings evil things out of the evil stored up in his heart. For the mouth speaks what the heart is full of."
>
> LUKE 6:45

The useful lesson is to live a life without guile and hatred and beware of flattering words from enemies especially those who have mastered the art of deception to cover the malice and hatred in their hearts. An adage says to keep your enemy close, this is the craftiness certain people of the world follow to know the strength and weaknesses of their opponents. Deceitful people keep up appearances and speak lies to mislead the innocent into thinking they are loyal friends, so, Believers should be vigilant in discerning deceitful friendships and assess everyone.

> "Beware of your friends; do not trust anyone in your clan. For every one of them is a deceiver, and every friend a slanderer."
>
> JEREMIAH 9:4

The Bible says the heart of men is treacherously wicked who can know it except God. It is therefore important to watch one's heart, to prevent the sin of hatred, malice and lies. And to test every spirit as advised by John.

"The heart is deceitful above all things, and it is extremely sick, who can understand it fully *and* know its secret motives?"

JEREMIAH 17:9

"Beloved, do not believe every spirit [speaking through a self-proclaimed prophet]; instead test the spirits to see whether they are from God, because many false prophets *and* teachers have gone out into the world."

1 JOHN 4:1

PRAYER

Dear Lord, we thank you for your word that offers protection against hatred and deceitful attacks of liars. We pray for your help to discern true friendships, so we can separate from enemies and remove people who are against us in Jesus' name. Amen.

CHAPTER 26

Godly Wealth and Riches

> "The blessing of the LORD brings wealth, without painful toil for it."
>
> PROVERBS 10:22

The Bible says it is the blessing of God, the empowerment of the Holy Spirit and the favour of God that makes people rich. This means it is God that gives people the power, wisdom, and the ability to gain wealth. The wisdom nugget, therefore, is to trust God for wealth and riches. And work hard but smartly for it, not toiling but through wise work, trade, and investment.

Riches should not be acquired through hardships, struggle, crime or at the expense of the Believer's health and wellbeing. So, Believers should trust God as their source of wealth and provisions, using the principle of multiplication to gain wealth. The Bible says God teaches his people how to become rich and successful.

> "Remember the LORD your God. He is the one who gives you the power to succeed to fulfil the covenant he confirmed to your ancestors with an oath."
>
> DEUTERONOMY 8:18

From the preceding scripture, one can conclude that God empowers his people to become successful and wealthy in life, so, the Believer should acknowledge God as their source as they do life to become prosperous. The scripture says God gives the Believer, favour, empowerment, talents, skills, creativity, intellect, and witty ideas which amount to the power required to become wealthy.

> **"Then the LORD said to Moses, "Look, I have specifically chosen Bezalel son of Uri, grandson of Hur, of the tribe of Judah. I have filled him with the Spirit of God, giving him great wisdom, ability, and expertise in all kinds of crafts. He is a master craftsman, an expert in working with gold, silver, and bronze. He is skilled in engraving and mounting gemstones and carving wood. He is a master at every craft!"**
>
> EXODUS 31:1-5

God empowers his people and makes a covenant of blessing with them. God blessed Abraham in the Book of Genesis, and he became very rich.

> **"I will make you into a great nation. I will bless you and make you famous, and you will be a blessing to others."**
>
> GENESIS 12:2

> **"Now Abram was extremely rich in livestock, silver and gold."**
>
> GENESIS 13:2

Some readers may be asking the question: "If it is God who empowers his people to gain wealth, why is it that the bulk of the world's economy and wealth is controlled by nonbelievers (those who do not know or believe in the existence of God)?" God is not a respecter of persons, his principles for wealth are embedded in the word of God, the Bible, and work for whoever applies them to their career or business. The wisdom will work for anyone who is shrewd like the shrewd servant.

Jesus told the story of the shrewd servant who was unfaithful in his dealings, so the master wanted to let him off his role as his manager. He applied shrewdness and approached all his master's debtors, he negotiated and made deals with them, reducing their debt to gain their favour. The Bible says his master was pleased with the manager's witty idea and praised him for being shrewd in his method to secure his future. Even though his method was dishonest, God justified him.

Jesus Explains Why the Worldly Gain Riches – The Parable of the Shrewd Manager

> "And his master commended the unjust manager [not for his misdeeds, but] because he had acted shrewdly [by preparing for his future unemployment]; for the sons of this age [the non-believers] are shrewder in relation to their own kind {that is, to the ways of the secular world] than are the sons of light [the believers]."
>
> LUKE 16:8

However, it is useful to mention that there are two kinds of riches, godly riches gained by righteous means and ungodly mammon acquired by violence. The godly wealth makes a person happy with no toiling, struggling or sorrow, whereas the ungodly wealth brings sorrow and pain with worry, stress, violence, fear, and anxiety. The Bible says not to envy those with unrighteous riches because they will suffer the consequences of their evil ways at judgement time (Proverbs 23:17). Godly riches are the recommended type of wealth to enjoy on earth for Believers. Ill-gotten wealth may be tempting because they seem easy and faster to obtain, but the end is destruction and vexation of the spirit.

A man called Job in the Bible asked the question, why do the wicked live on and increase in power (Job 21:7). Whilst the answer may be one of God's mysteries, Jesus Christ attempted an answer in Matthew 13 in his parables on the kingdom of God.

The Parable of the Weeds

"He put another parable before them, saying, "The kingdom of heaven may be compared to a man who sowed good seed in his field, but while his men were sleeping, his enemy came and sowed weeds among the wheat and went away. So, when the plants came up and bore grain, then the weeds appeared also. And the servants of the master of the house came and said to him, 'Master, did you not sow good seed in your field? How then does it have weeds?' He said to them, 'An enemy has done this. So, the servants said to him, 'Then do you want us to go and gather them?' But he said, 'No, lest in gathering the weeds you root up the wheat along with them. Let both grow together until the harvest, and at harvest time I will tell the reapers, "Gather the weeds first and bind them in bundles to be burned but gather the wheat into my barn.""

MATTHEW 13:24-30

The parable of the weeds gives a glimpse into the destruction that awaits the wicked. So, the Bible warns not to envy them, even if they seem to prosper here on earth.

"For I was envious of the arrogant, as I saw the prosperity of the wicked."

PSALM 73:3

"Be still before the LORD; wait patiently for Him *and* entrust yourself to Him; Do not fret (whine, agonize) because of him who prospers in his way, because of the man who carries out wicked schemes."

PSALM 37:7

Apostle Paul confirmed in his teachings that there will be judgement, so, one must be conscious of that fact, and put things into proper perspective, in the way one lives, particularly in the arena of business, success and wealth. The final take is to let one's wealth foundation be based on wise and godly principles.

Wealth should be based upon the principles of God's word which is based on love. Riches must never be gained by methods which harm people or the planet. Christians should remember that judgement day will come one day, so, as the Bible teaches, they should always bear in mind that it is the Lord their God that can help them obtain godly riches with no sorrow or regret.

> **"For we must all stand before Christ to be judged. We will each receive whatever we deserve for the good or evil we have done in this earthly body."**
>
> 2 CORINTHIANS 5:10

PRAYER

Our Father who art in heaven, we praise you! We ask for godly wealth and pray for your empowerment and favour with people to help us succeed in our careers and profit in our businesses in Jesus' name. Amen.

CHAPTER 27

Fear, Faith, and Positive Thinking

> *"The fears of the wicked will be fulfilled; the hopes of the godly will be granted."*
>
> PROVERBS 10:24

The wisdom nugget of this scripture is to think faith-filled, positive, and pure thoughts and have godly desires. People's nightmares come true, and those who dwell on the fear of evil or entertain evil thoughts have their thoughts materialise. The antidote to fear and nightmare is Faith and love. Faith in God conquers all human fear, and the love of God overcomes fear.

The story of Job in the Book of Job is an example of the consequences of fearing evil. Job was fearful about his children sinning and offending God. He feared evil might come upon them as a result, his nightmare happened, and all his children died. And he exclaimed that his fears have come true!

> *"What I always feared has happened to me. What I dreaded has come true."*
>
> JOB 3:25

Job was always afraid of God's judgement forgetting that God is a good God whose love is steadfast and new each morning. The Bible says God is a good and faithful God whose love is eternal. But Job focused solely on the God who smites, forgetting that God is a Merciful God who forgives sin. His lack of faith and trust in God concerning his children landed him in his worst nightmares, everything he possessed crashed around him because the devil tested him, to see if he would curse God.

Job lived life from a position of fear which is the opposite of love and faith. He failed to distinguish between fear of the Devil and holy fear of God based upon the love and mercy of God Almighty. He often offered sacrifices to appease God just in case his children sinned during their parties. His efforts focused on fear of satanic attacks rather than faith in God's protection.

> **"Job's sons would take turns preparing feasts in their homes, and they would also invite their three sisters to celebrate with them. When these celebrations ended—sometimes after several days—Job would purify his children. He would get up early in the morning and offer a burnt offering for each of them. For Job said to himself, "Perhaps my children have sinned and have cursed God in their hearts." This was Job's regular practice."**
>
> JOB 1:4-5

Job's way of doing life in fear is contrary to God's recommendation for his people, which is to live in faith and love. Believers should, therefore, have faith and trust God and never entertain fears. The Bible says the Just shall live by faith not by law because the law can no longer deliver, as Job found out when his sacrifices for his children, failed to keep them alive.

> **"Now it is clear that no one is justified before God by the law, because "The righteous will live by faith.""**
>
> GALATIANS 3:11

The righteous who live by faith in God need not fear because God is with them. The Believer's heart desires should therefore be based on things they want from God or the aspirations they want to see happen, not the things they do not want to see manifest in their lives. Faith is therefore, believing and hoping for the best, not preparing for the worst. The Bible defines faith as the evidence of things not yet seen but hoped for.

> **"Now faith is the assurance (title deed, confirmation) of things hoped for (divinely guaranteed), and the evidence of things not seen [the conviction of their reality—faith comprehends as fact what cannot be experienced by the physical senses]."**
>
> HEBREWS 1:11

Prayer requests should be in a format that hangs upon faith. Believers should pray in faith asking for things they like to see happen in their lives. No one should spend their time praying against what they do not want or wish to happen. An example is not to pray against accidents or death in one's daily prayer, instead, one should ask for long life and God's divine protection and make declarations accordingly.

Examples of Positive Faith-Filled Prayers

> "For he will order his angels to protect you wherever you go."
>
> PSALM 91:11

> "I will not die, but live, and declare the works *and* recount the illustrious acts of the LORD."
>
> PSALM 118:17

Remember, the Lord has not given us a spirit of fear but of love, power, and a sound mind to do great and mighty deeds.

God Gives the Spirit of Love, not of Fear

> "For God did not give us a spirit of timidity *or* cowardice *or* fear, but [He has given us a spirit] of power and love and of sound judgment *and* personal discipline [abilities that result in a calm, well-balanced mind, and self-control]."
>
> 2 TIMOTHY 1:7

In other words, heart desires and prayer requests should be positive, faith-filled and inspired by love, never negativity, evil or fear. Apostle Paul suggested how to achieve a faith-filled lifestyle in his letter to the Philippians.

> "And now, dear brothers and sisters, one final thing. Fix your thoughts on what is true, honourable, right, pure, lovely, and admirable. Think about things that are excellent and worthy of praise."
>
> PHILIPPIANS 4:8

This still goes back to the foundation of the human soul, the heart. The Bible says whatever a person thinks about, they attract or become because thoughts can attract good or terrible things. The Believer must therefore pay attention to their thoughts because thoughts can impact their life either negatively or positively.

Christians, rather than fearing the evils of tomorrow, should live their lives fearlessly, living each day courageously in faith, believing in God for a good future and trusting him with hope for a great life. Bill and Gloria Gaither in their Hymn; Because He lives, declare Christians can face the future, without worry because Jesus is alive, and he owns the future. Hallelujah!

God's instruction to Joshua when he selected him as the leader to replace Moses is to be courageous and fearless. Courage gives the strength, necessary to achieve success. Fear is a weakness that hinders progress, it prevents people from fulfilling their heart desires. Joshua believed in God and lived a successful and courageous life. Through his fearless leadership, God fulfilled his promises to the Israelites.

> **"This is my command—be strong and courageous! Do not be afraid or discouraged. For the LORD, your God is with you wherever you go."**
>
> JOSHUA 1:9

> **"Not one of all the LORD's good promises to Israel failed; everyone was fulfilled."**
>
> JOSHUA 21:45

So, to see every good desire fulfilled, be not afraid, be strong and trust in God. He is a helper who promises to help his people overcome life challenges and the attacks of the devil. Whilst Believers do not fear evil, they are to do life in the holy fear of God, holding him in awe because he is a formidable God who fulfils every good desire of his people within his will.

> **"He grants the desires of those who fear him; he hears their cries for help and rescues them"**
>
> PSALM 145:19

PRAYER

Dear Lord, we ask for the strength to courageously do life without any fears in Jesus' name. Amen.

CHAPTER 28

Slothfulness and Laziness

> "Lazy people irritate their employers, like vinegar to the teeth or smoke in the eyes."
>
> PROVERBS 10:26

The wisdom nugget is to be diligent because a lazy person is an irritation to their employer or people in general. Proverbs 6:6 instructs the people of God to follow the diligent behaviour of the Ant. Apostle Paul wrote that Believers should never be slothful in their work.

> "Never be lazy but work hard and serve the Lord enthusiastically."
>
> ROMANS 12:11

Jesus Christ condemned laziness and likened it to wickedness in the parable of the Talent. The master in the story, gave talents to his servants to manage and multiply but one of them hid his talent. The master called him a wicked servant when he returned. He took the talent from him and gave it to the servant using his talents and taking calculated risks to multiply them. This implies God will bless those who live their lives fearlessly taking calculated risks financially.

Jesus' Teaching About Slothfulness – The Parable of the Talents

> "I was afraid I would lose your money, so I hid it in the earth. Look, here is your money back. "But the master replied, 'You wicked and lazy servant! If you knew I harvested crops I did not plant and gathered crops I did not cultivate, why didn't you deposit my money in the bank? At least I could have gotten some interest. Then, he ordered, 'Take the money from this servant, and give it to the one with the ten bags of silver on it."
>
> MATTHEW 25:25-28

Fear is usually the excuse given by lazy people, rather than taking responsibility for their lives and laying hold of God's promises through courage and faith, they hide their talents and skills and go about life, doing nothing, and blaming others who are doing well. The wisdom to a successful life is hard and smart work. Fear is an emotion that Believers must overcome, it should never become an excuse to fail.

Proverbs 26:13 says the sluggard says there is a lion in the way, there is a lion on the streets, so, they stay at home and sleep rather than go out to engage in profitable work. It is my prayer that every reader will do life valiantly with courage and determination like the wise servant who multiplied his five talents or the one who multiplied his two talents.

It does not matter how big or small one's talent is, what matters is whether it makes one's life better and prosperous through the wisdom of multiplication and smart work. Life's efforts are often about multiplication and smart working to achieve success and gain prosperity. God bless the work of those who are diligent in their work.

> "The LORD will send rain at the proper time from his rich treasury in the heavens and will bless all the work you do. You will lend to many nations, but you will never need to borrow from them."
>
> DEUTERONOMY 28:12

> "And God can bless you abundantly, so that in all things at all times, having all that you need, you will abound in every good work."
>
> 2 CORINTHIANS 9:8

King Solomon in his writing says to do whatever work you do passionately. Apostle Paul advised Christians to do their work diligently as unto God.

> "Work willingly at whatever you do, as though you were working for the Lord rather than for people."
>
> COLOSSIANS 3:23

> "Whatever you do, do well. For when you go to the grave, there will be no work or planning or knowledge or wisdom."
>
> ECCLESIASTES 9:10

PRAYER

Father, we pray for strength and the grace to be diligent in our work in Jesus' name. Amen

CHAPTER 29

Long Life

> "The [reverent] fear of the LORD [worshipping, obeying, serving, and trusting Him with awe-filled respect] prolongs one's life, but the years of the wicked will be shortened."
>
> PROVERBS 10:27

The fear of God is holy respect for God, loving him and obeying his commandment. The Bible promises the reward of long life for those who do life with love, those who love God and pay attention to his commandments, so as not to offend him or sin against him. God's principle of love teaches Christians to love God wholeheartedly and show love to everyone. The wisdom nugget is therefore to fear God and obey his commandments for the reward of long and vibrant life.

> **"Therefore, be careful to obey every command I am giving you today, so you may have the strength to go in and take over the land you are about to enter. If you obey, you will enjoy a long life in the land the LORD swore to give to your ancestors to you, their descendants—a land flowing with milk and honey!"**
>
> DEUTERONOMY 11:8-9

The fear of God is the beginning of understanding. The fear of God helps the Believer live righteously through obedience to God's law. Jesus said if you love me, you will obey my commandments (John 14:15).

There is a reward of long life for those who follow God's instructions. They get a covenant and promise of life, which is an enjoyment of long life and eternal life.

> "I will reward them with a long life and give them my salvation."
>
> PSALM 91:16

> "My covenant with Levi was [one of] life and peace, and I gave them to him as an object of reverence; so, he [and the priests] feared Me and stood in reverent awe of My name."
>
> MALACHI 2:5

PRAYER

Grant us long life O Lord, in Jesus' name, we pray. Amen.

CHAPTER 30

Ambition and Achievement

> *"The hopes of the godly result in happiness, but the expectations of the wicked come to nothing."*
>
> PROVERBS 10:28

The wisdom nugget of this scripture is to be good and righteous to receive the reward of achievement of life aspirations. The Bible says the hopes of good people come true, and they have joy and happiness. Simply put, God satisfies the desires of righteous people and help them to succeed and achieve their ambition.

> **"Take delight in the LORD, and he will give you your heart's desires."**
>
> PSALM 37:4

The question is how does one become good when Jesus said that no one is good except God the Father (Mark 10:18)? Believers should always think of loving and obeying God, then love and respect other people. Jesus used the Parable of the Good Samaritan (Luke 10:25-37) to illustrate his teaching on the qualities of a good person.

In the story, a man whom the Bible called the Good Samaritan, took care of a stranger who was robbed and left for dead during a journey. Passers-by including a priest ignored the man, but the Good Samaritan helped him. Jesus concluded the good person is the one who showed the man compassion even though he was a stranger.

The Bible says those who do wickedly will have their hopes and expectations cut off, they will not achieve their ambition. Christians should therefore, pay attention to living righteously. However, they should not depend on their own righteousness as the Pharisees and hypocrites do. They should emulate Jesus Christ and follow his good examples of love and humility because it is God that ascribes righteousness to his people by faith and by works.

One can conclude that it is faith in Jesus demonstrated through works that make a person good. So, good requires a physical act of love and a show of kindness to fellow human beings. Faith in Jesus Christ, obedience to God's commandments and charitable deeds to fellow human beings including strangers are the criteria for becoming a good follower of Jesus Christ. That is what makes a person great, and the rewards are success, fulfilled dreams and aspirations. Whereas those who do wickedly will have their aspirations frustrated.

> **"You will be rewarded for this; your hope will not be disappointed."**
>
> PROVERBS 23:18

> **"Then men will say, "There is surely a reward for the righteous! There is surely a God who judges the earth!"**
>
> PSALM 58:11

PRAYER

Dear Lord, we pray for the grace to live a righteous life. We ask that you grant us the strength to be obedient to your commandments, so that our hopes and aspirations can succeed in Jesus' name. Amen.

CHAPTER 31

Honesty in Business

> *"The LORD detests the use of dishonest scales,*
> *but he delights in accurate weights."*
>
> PROVERBS 11:1

This is the guideline to follow for those in business. The wisdom nugget is to be people of integrity and not to be dishonest in business dealings. Whilst the scripture deals with dishonest scales for measuring quantities of products sold, it applies to every aspect of life.

> **"Your scales and weights must be accurate. Your containers for measuring dry materials or liquids must be accurate. I am the LORD your God who brought you out of the land of Egypt."**
>
> LEVITICUS 19:36

God will not tolerate cheating and deceit in any form. Everyone should live in a just manner, ensuring fairness in every action taken that affects the lives of other people, financially or otherwise. The Bible says God finds dishonesty despicable, so the lesson is to do life with integrity and honesty.

> "For everyone who does such things, everyone who acts unjustly [without personal integrity] is utterly repulsive to the LORD your God."
>
> DEUTERONOMY 25:16

It may sometimes be tempting to cheat in life because it appears to be the faster way to achieve success, particularly riches and money. But the Bible warns the people of God against fraudulent ways because it creates lustful desires that can derail the Believer from the path of righteousness.

> "And what do you benefit if you gain the whole world but lose your soul? Is anything worth more than your soul?"
>
> MARK 8:36-37

It is worth noting that God is a Merciful God who forgives, blesses, and restores his people if they regret their past sins and repent. So, if anyone is currently cheating in their business affairs, they can change their way. The Bible story of Jacob offers hope to whoever is currently cheating. His experience demonstrates God forgives his people whenever they repent and change their ways of doing life.

God transformed Jacob from a cheater to a blessed man. His name meant deceiver, he cheated his brother Esau of his birthright blessings and fled. But God changed his name from Jacob, the deceiver to Israel, the Blessed.

> "God said to him, "Your name is Jacob, but you will no longer be called Jacob; your name will be Israel. So, he named him Israel."
>
> GENESIS 35:10

PRAYER

Dear Lord, we give you thanks for your word and commandments. We pray for the power to gain honest wealth in Jesus' name. Amen.

CHAPTER 32

Godly People and a Nation's Prosperity

> "By the blessing [of the influence] of the upright the city is exalted, but by the mouth of the wicked it is torn down."
>
> PROVERBS 11:11

The wisdom nugget in this scripture is, good citizens, build their cities. Good people who are doing well in life will help the city grow and develop, the wicked will do life and speak in a manner that brings curses and ruin to their city. The Bible says when the righteous thrive, the people rejoice, but not so for the wicked.

> **"The whole city celebrates when the godly succeed; they shout for joy when the wicked die."**
>
> PROVERBS 11:10

A good illustration is the story of Joseph, he was a godly and wise man whom King Pharoah employed as the governor of Egypt, to administer food and provision, and to maintain the nation's economy through the seven years of prosperity and famine. He was a man in whom there was the Spirit of God, hence the nation prospered and was rescued from the famine dreamt by the king (Genesis 41).

> **"So, Pharaoh asked his officials, "Can we find anyone else like this man so obviously filled with the spirit of God? Then Pharaoh said to Joseph, "Since God has revealed the meaning of the dreams to you, clearly no one else is as intelligent or wise as you are."**
>
> GENESIS 41:38-39

PRAYER

Father, we pray for our nations, we ask that you appoint great and wise leaders filled with the Spirit of God like Joseph to build and make our nations and the people prosperous in Jesus' name. Amen.

CHAPTER 33

Give Good Work and Negotiate a Good Pay

> "The wicked man earns deceptive wages, but he who sows righteousness and lives his life with integrity will have a true reward [that is both permanent and satisfying]."
>
> PROVERBS 11:18

The wisdom nugget is to provide a decent job in exchange for a good wage. This means providing value and getting a well-deserved monetary reward for goods or services. Excellent work deserves good pay, which means everyone should expect a decent salary in exchange for their skills and talents or a fair price for quality products sold.

There is a world adage that says if you pay peanuts, you will get monkeys which translates to the fact that paying low wages will attract unskilled workers. Jacob whilst living with his uncle Laban worked hard but did not get a reward for his work until he demanded and negotiated payments for his labour as a shepherd.

Negotiating good pay and setting a fair price by the level of work, services or goods provided is, therefore, a godly way to conduct business and career.

Jacob Negotiated a Good Wage for His Labour

"You had little indeed before I came, but your wealth has increased enormously. The LORD has blessed you through everything I have done. But now, what about me? When can I start providing for my own family?

What wages do you want? **Laban** asked again.

Jacob replied: Do not give me anything. Just do this one thing, and I will continue to tend and watch over your flocks. Let me inspect your flocks today and remove all the sheep and goats that are speckled or spotted, along with all the black sheep.

Give these to me as my wages."

GENESIS 30:30-32

The Bible says Jacob became so prosperous from the good wages he obtained in exchange for his labour, that his cousins became jealous of his achievement. They accused him of stealing their father's wealth.

"But Jacob soon learned that Laban's sons were grumbling about him. Jacob has robbed our father of everything, they said. "He has gained all his wealth at our father's expense."

GENESIS 31:1

PRAYER

Dear Lord, we ask for a good wage in exchange for the labour we provide and a good profit for those in business in Jesus' name. Amen.

CHAPTER 34

Generosity – Be Generous!

> "There is the one who [generously] scatters [abroad], and yet increases all the more and there is the one who withholds what is justly due, but it results only in want and poverty."
>
> PROVERBS 11:24

The wisdom nugget of this Proverb is to be generous givers. The Bible promotes generosity because giving reproduces after its kind. The Bible says whatever a man sows (gives) that he will receive in multiple folds.

> **"Give, and you will receive. Your gift will return to you in full, pressed down, shaken together to make room for more, running over, and poured into your lap. The amount you give will determine the amount you get back."**
>
> LUKE 6:38

Generosity usually bears the fruit of wealth. There is always a return on investment provided the giver is obedient to God's will and listens to the inspiration of the Holy Spirit. Givers need to carefully select a worthy cause or charity to sow into. The Bible repeatedly says; that whatever a person sows he will reap. Whilst the scripture is meant to teach about sowing spiritual things to reap eternal life, the same wisdom can apply to gifts.

> "Do not be deceived, God is not mocked [He will not allow Himself to be ridiculed, nor treated with contempt nor allow His precepts to be scornfully set aside]; for whatever a man sows, this *and* this only is what he will reap."
>
> GALATIANS 6:7

Therefore, Christians should be generous people sharing their wealth with others particularly the poor and those of the household of God. The Bible says thieves and those who do not work, should work, so they can have surplus provisions for themselves and others less privileged than themselves.

> "So then, while we [as individual believers] have the opportunity, let us do good to all people [not only being helpful, but also doing that which promotes their spiritual well-being], and especially [be a blessing] to those of the household of faith (born-again believers)."
>
> GALATIANS 6:10

> "The thief [who has become a believer] must no longer steal, but instead he must work hard [making an honest living], producing that which is good with his own hands, so that he will have *something* to share with those in need."
>
> EPHESIANS 4:28

Doing life in a great manner requires the ability to share one's wealth. Generosity is a gift of the Holy Spirit, some people find it easy to give than others but whatever level a Believer is, the wisdom is to learn to give and consider giving as an investment that will generate a future reward.

Whilst giving generously is a good thing, abuse can happen when one is unwise in their giving. It is, therefore, necessary to add a word of caution; wicked people sometimes use pretentious situations to swindle and defraud generous people of their wealth. So, Believers should be careful with their giving and apply wisdom to discern where to give their money. Christians should give carefully with the leading of the Holy Spirit who can decide what causes to give to because giving done foolishly is not charity.

That said, it is good to know that giving generously has great rewards for the Believer. The benefit of generosity is prosperity. God repays the money given to the poor because he who gives to the poor lends to God (Proverbs 19:17). The Holy Spirit compensates and inspires other people to favour or give back to the giver. There is the adage that givers never lack, those who bless others, are refreshed by others as well. The Bible concludes the giver will get back with the same measure with which he gives.

> **"Now [remember] this: he who sows sparingly will also reap sparingly, and he who sows generously [that blessings may come to others] will also reap generously [and be blessed]."**
>
> 2 CORINTHIANS 9:6

> **"The generous will prosper; those who refresh others will themselves be refreshed."**
>
> PROVERBS 11:25

> **"Those who give to the poor will lack nothing, but those who close their eyes to them receive many curses."**
>
> PROVERBS 28:27

PRAYER

Father, we thank you for your wisdom on how to do life generously, we ask for the gift of generosity in Jesus' name. Amen.

CHAPTER 35

Trust in God, not in Riches!

> "He who leans on and trusts in and is confident in his riches will fall, But the righteous [who trust in God's provision] will flourish like a green leaf."
>
> PROVERBS 11:28

The wisdom nugget is to trust in God as the source of one's provisions. To do life otherwise brings destruction because one's focus shifts to money and self-confidence. Dependence upon God shapes the Believer's life into life fully devoted to God not worldly things. Trusting in money brings vanity upon a person which ends up destroying such a person.

However, the question is; does this scripture mean people should not pursue wealth? The Bible clearly states God gives his people the power to gain wealth (Deuteronomy 8:18). God wants his people to be rich but not to depend or focus on their wealth. Timothy clarified this further in the Book of Timothy.

> "Teach those who are rich in this world not to be proud and not to trust in their money, which is so unreliable. Their trust should be in God, who richly gives us all we need for our enjoyment."
>
> 1 TIMOTHY 6:17

Timothy explained in the preceding scripture not to trust in riches but to consider God the source of all things. God is the creator and provider who gives all things to his people to enjoy. He hates people who idolise or worship riches. But he loves those who love him, and him alone, treating everything else as secondary.

Trusting in the name of the Lord is, therefore, the key to a flourishing and prosperous life. No man can serve two masters; therefore, a Believer cannot do life with a combination of serving God and Money as equal masters. The Believer must never trust in the power of money for their provision nor the strength of horses for their protection.

> "No one can serve two masters. For you will hate one and love the other; you will be devoted to one and despise the other. You cannot serve God and be enslaved to money."
>
> MATTHEW 6:24

> "Some trust in chariots and some in horses, but we trust in the name of the LORD our God."
>
> PSALM 20:7

PRAYER

Our Father in heaven, we pray for the grace to trust you wholeheartedly as our source. We ask for the strength and discipline to consider money as an ordinary tool in Jesus' name. Amen.

God is Our Source!

CHAPTER 36

Do Not Exploit or Abuse Your Family

> *"Those who bring trouble on their families inherit the wind. The fool will be a servant to the wise."*
>
> PROVERBS 11:29

The wisdom nugget in this scripture is not to abuse or exploit members of your household. Abuse is taking advantage, mismanaging, or maltreating people or things. It is an exploitation of people, using them for selfish purposes, those who do so, are people users. The Bible commands the people of God to owe no one nothing but love. This law applies most especially to people of the same household. Family members must not exploit each other or engage in matters that will harm other members of the family.

> **"Owe nothing to anyone except to love *and* seek the best for one another; for he who [unselfishly] loves his neighbour has fulfilled the [essence of the] law [relating to one's fellowman]."**
>
> ROMANS 13:8

The lesson is to love one's fellow human beings, particularly those of one's household. There are consequences for those who behave in a way that harms their friends and family. The Bible says they will become servants to those who are wise enough to obey the law of love.

PRAYER

Father Lord, we pray that Christians will mature in their mental attitude and emotions and live wisely, loving and respecting their family members in Jesus' name. Amen.

CHAPTER 37

The Power of Words

> "The words of the wicked are like a murderous ambush, but the words of the godly save lives."
>
> PROVERBS 12:6

The wisdom nugget is to use words that build and edify people and not slander people. Malicious and spiteful words harm others, they are despicable to God. It is God's will for Christians to live peacefully with fellow human beings. Therefore, Believers should avoid unwholesome speeches that harm other people because that will be contrary to the law of love.

> "Do not use foul or abusive language. Let everything you say be good and helpful so that your words will be an encouragement to those who hear them."
>
> EPHESIANS 4:29

> "Nor should there be obscenity, foolish talk, or crude joking, which are out of character, but rather thanksgiving."
>
> EPHESIANS 5:4

> "But now you must put aside all such things as these: anger, rage, malice, slander, and filthy language from your lips."
>
> COLOSSIANS 3:8

> "Let your speech always be gracious, seasoned with salt, so that you may know how to answer everyone."
>
> COLOSSIANS 4:6

The wisdom is to watch what comes out of the mouth and ensure all speeches are holy and pure. Christians must speak only the words that bless and uplift others. The Bible teaches Believers to pay attention to their lips and guard their mouths against destructive words.

> "Out of the same mouth come *both* blessing and cursing. These things, my brothers, should not be this way [for we have a moral obligation to speak in a manner that reflects our fear of God and profound respect for His precepts]."
>
> JAMES 3:10

Apostle Paul says the secret of good speeches is keeping the heart pure, focusing on things that are worthy of praise (Philippians 4:8), and meditating on the word of God because it is from the content of the heart that the mouth will speak. Jesus confirms the importance of maintaining a good heart because out of the abundance of the heart, the mouth speaks.

> "You brood of vipers, how can you who are evil say anything good? For out of the overflow of the heart, the mouth speaks."
>
> MATTHEW 12:34

It is, therefore, essential for good living, for the Believer to watch their speeches, and speak words of affirmation, that help, inspire, encourage, and build others up. Believers must choose comforting and productive words that promote the well-being and peace of mind of fellow human beings rather than malicious hateful words.

Believers' beautiful and uplifting words will ensure peaceful living with their neighbours. It is best to remain quiet if one has nothing good to say that will build people up.

> **"So then, let us pursue [with enthusiasm] the things which make for peace and the building up of one another [things which lead to spiritual growth]."**
>
> ROMANS 14:19

PRAYER

Dear Lord, we pray for the grace to do life peacefully, paying attention to our mouths. Give us the grace to speak only blessings and never curses in Jesus' name. Amen.

CHAPTER 38

Righteousness and a Happy Home

> "The wicked are overthrown [by their evil] and are no more, But the house of the [consistently] righteous will stand [securely]."
>
> PROVERBS 12:7

The wisdom nugget of this scripture is to live a righteous life to enjoy a peaceful and happy home. The Bible says no matter what goes on in the world, your place of habitation shall be safe, and your household will live securely. Proverbs 14:11 further expatiate this wisdom nugget proclaiming the house of the wicked will be overthrown, whilst the tabernacle of the upright shall flourish. And the Book of Job says God will give the pure-hearted a content home.

> "And if you are pure and live with integrity, he will surely rise and restore your happy home."
>
> JOB 8:6

The Bible teaches that righteousness is a useful tool to live a prosperous life, so, Christians should live righteously to enjoy an abundant and prosperous life. Living life righteously brings glory to God, it has the reward of happiness and security. The Lord will protect, provide, and give peace to people who live by God's word, the Bible, and those who follow the examples of his son Jesus Christ. Those who live righteously will have their path shine to the glory of God.

> **"But the path of the just *is* as the shining light, that shineth more and more unto the perfect day."**
>
> PROVERBS 4:18

PRAYER

Dear Lord, we thank you for your love and protection over the righteous. We pray for the Holy Spirit to keep us on the path of righteousness to enjoy a happy and peaceful home in Jesus' name. Amen.

CHAPTER 39

The Integrity of Work

> *"Better to be a nobody and yet have a servant than pretend to be somebody and have no food."*
>
> PROVERBS 12:9

The wisdom nugget is not to think too highly of oneself at the expense of earning an honest living. To humble oneself and take up any work for a fair wage to pay one's household bills is the recommended righteous way of living. It is best to take up any wage-paying work rather than pretend to be someone of importance and boastfully honour oneself without the necessary finances to do so. Those who live in that manner have been known to end in misery and poverty.

This scripture promotes the integrity of honest work. Timothy encourages Christians to work for their living. Earning an honest living is much better than starving or begging others for money to pay for living expenses.

> *"Anyone who does not provide for their relatives, and especially for their household, has denied the faith and is worse than an unbeliever."*
>
> 1 TIMOTHY 5:8

Pretending to be a big person whilst one is not, means one is a liar and a deluded pompous fraudster deceiving their own self. Such a person is considered lazy and self-destructive to their own survival and that of their relatives. Furthermore, the Bible ascribes pride to such behaviour and the consequences are financial struggles, poverty, begging, stealing, cheating and failure. Such behaviour has the consequences of an eventual disgrace and humiliation from other people.

Those who act important rather than work will suffer humiliation and ridicule when begging others for food. The Bible says the righteous will never beg for food because they will work and trust God for their daily needs.

> "Once I was young, and now I am old. Yet I have never seen the godly abandoned or their children begging for bread."
>
> PSALM 37:25

PRAYER

O Lord, we ask that you grant us the grace to live a humble life. Give us the humility and courage to earn a decent and an honest living. We pray for the power to gain wealth and live honestly with integrity rather than live a pompous and arrogant life that tends only to poverty and shame in Jesus' name. Amen.

CHAPTER 40

Good People are Good to Their Animals

> *"The godly care for their animals, but the wicked are always cruel."*
>
> PROVERBS 12:10

The wisdom is to be kind to animals. This is asking animal owners to take care of the needs of their animals, to feed and water them according to the needs of their kind. Deuteronomy 25:4 says not to muzzle the ox when he treads out the corn. So, the Bible wants animal owners to be kind and take care of their animals.

God notices and sees everything humans do, so the fact that animals cannot complain, or talk does not mean the wicked will get away with animal abuse. A notable example is the story of the donkey maltreated by Balaam in the Bible. The Lord opened the donkey's mouth and he spoke in condemnation of its maltreatment.

God intervened when Balaam Maltreated his Donkey

"Then the LORD gave the donkey the ability to speak. "What have I done to you that deserves your beating me three times?" it asked Balaam.

"You have made me look like a fool!" Balaam shouted. "If I had a sword with me, I would kill you!"

"But I am the same donkey you have ridden all your life," the donkey answered. "Have I ever done anything like this before?"

"No," Balaam admitted. Then the LORD opened Balaam's eyes, and he saw the angel of the LORD standing in the roadway with a drawn sword in his hand. Balaam bowed his head and fell face down on the ground before him.

"Why did you beat your donkey those three times?" the angel of the LORD demanded. "Look, I have come to block your way because you are stubbornly resisting me."

NUMBERS 22:28-32

The lesson to draw from Balaam's interaction with the angel over his abuse of his donkey is simply to be kind to all living things, so, as not to have one's path obstructed by God. Compassion and kindness are part of the criteria that are necessary for living a godly and happy life. Whether to human beings, animals, or any of God's creations, Christians ought to show mercy.

PRAYER

Dear Lord, we pray that you help every Believer to be kind and compassionate, showing kindness to all people and animals in Jesus' name. Amen.

CHAPTER 41

Stay on the Job – Only the Witless Chase Whims and Fancies

> *"Those who work their land will have abundant food, but those who chase fantasies have no sense."*
>
> PROVERBS 12:11

The wisdom nugget is to be hardworking and earn a good and honest living rather than chase fantasies and useless ideas that never come to anything good. This scripture is correcting people who go about life with unimaginable ideas, never committing to any profitable career or business. They live off other people's efforts and swindle their way throughout life.

Those who live this way usually die of poverty and shame. Therefore, this wisdom nugget should serve as a wake-up call to repentance for those who have thus far lived life in laziness and fancies. Timothy tells Believers to engage in profitable work or business so that they can at least feed and provide for their own families (1 Timothy 5:8).

In other words, Believers should find useful and productive work to earn an honest wage. The Bible promises a reward of provision for those who engage in work, promising they will be successful and have their work established. They will reap a bountiful harvest and eat the fruit of their labour.

> "And may the Lord our God show us his approval and make our efforts successful. Yes, make our efforts successful!"
>
> PSALM 90:17

> "You will eat the fruit of your labour; blessings and prosperity will be yours."
>
> PSALM 128:2

PRAYER

Dear Lord, we ask for the grace to work smart and not chase or engage in foolish pursuits that do not profit us financially in Jesus' name. Amen.

CHAPTER 42

Be Teachable

> "The way of the [arrogant] fool [who rejects God's wisdom] is right in his own eyes, but a wise and prudent man is he who listens to counsel."
>
> PROVERBS 12:15

A fool is a person who acts unwisely, a silly person who disregards God's recommended ways of doing life. Foolish people are usually headstrong and stubborn, believing their ways are right, they live in delusion. Their folly and failure to seek wise counsel, eventually lead to their failure.

> "There is a way which seems right to a man *and* appears straight before him, but its end is the way of death."
>
> PROVERBS 16:25

On the other hand, a wise person lives carefully, seeking godly advice and following the instructions of God and wise people. Their path is filled with fewer mistakes, and they live wisely and successfully.

> **"The wise will hear and increase their learning, and the person of understanding will acquire wise counsel *and* the skill [to steer his course wisely and lead others to the truth]."**
>
> PROVERBS 1:5

Children and young people like to explore life. They forge their own path and stubbornly try new ways of doing things. Often, they make mistakes and through such mistakes, they gain harsh wisdom from real-life experiences. Through their trial and error and failures, they learn lessons useful for life. So, as they grow older, they become wiser, developing in wisdom, maturity, and sound judgement, thereby departing from their foolish and obstinate mindset.

> **"When I was a child, I spoke and thought and reasoned like a child. But when I grew up, I put away childish things."**
>
> 1 CORINTHIANS 13:11

The wisdom nugget of Proverbs 12:15 is, therefore, to seek and follow the godly counsel and to walk in obedience to God's word. Wise people are teachable, they listen to advice and do a self-reflection on how to do life better. They enjoy safety amidst wise counsellors (Proverbs 11:14). They enjoy a quicker path to success than headstrong people.

> **"For whoever has [a teachable heart], to him *more* [understanding] will be given; and whoever does not have [a yearning for truth], even what he has will be taken away from him."**
>
> MARK 4:25

PRAYER

Dear Lord, we pray for a teachable heart that seeks understanding and counsel for a better life and future. Grant us the will to follow godly instructions and surround us with wise counsellors in Jesus' name. Amen.

CHAPTER 43

Emotional Intelligence – Stay Calm!

> "A fool is quick-tempered, but a wise person stays calm when insulted."
>
> PROVERBS 12:16

The wisdom nugget is to exercise self-control over sudden outbursts of emotional anger. Self-control is part of the fruit of the Holy Spirit, it is having self-discipline and the ability to control one's emotions. A fool lacks the self-control to control their emotions of anger. So, rather than brush off insults, they burst into anger at every insult.

The Bible advises Christians to be quick to hear and slow to speak. So, a wise person will shrug off insults and walk away from unnecessary quarrels. An unwise outburst of anger usually leads people into the sin of resentment and unforgiveness which the Bible says will lead foolish people into self-destruction.

> "For anger slays the foolish man, and jealousy kills the simple (naive)."
>
> JOB 5:2

Believers should, therefore, learn to restrain and hold back their anger, harnessing every negative emotion that holds them back in life. To overcome the evils of anger, Believers should reflect wisely on how to resolve conflicts, trusting the Lord of Recompense who avenges his people.

PRAYER

Dear Lord, we give you thanks. We pray for the will and strength to be calm in the face of persecution and insults in Jesus' name. Amen.

CHAPTER 44

Truth and Keeping Promises

> "The LORD detests lying lips, but he delights in those who tell the truth."
>
> PROVERBS 12:22

The Bible says God loves truthful people, he hates liars, so, the wisdom nugget is to always speak the truth and maintain the integrity of your words. Believers should be people of integrity, with sincere and truthful speeches. Previous chapters have dealt with the need to pay attention to the lips and to watch over what goes into the heart because it will eventually come out of the mouth.

A Believer's words should be true and pure, spoken to fulfil promises. Words are powerful, so, Believer should not make reckless promises that will amount to lies. Underestimating or overestimating a situation or exaggeration can sometimes amount to lies. Believers can mislead or deceive people unintentionally, they should, therefore, weigh their words carefully, especially ones that deliver a promise.

God's words are Yes and Amen, they come to fulfilment. Therefore, he expects his children to keep their promises and speak only words that are useful and profitable to people. This scripture applies to words and promises made to God as well. The Bible warns it is better to stay silent than speak or make promises that one cannot fulfil.

> **"When you make a promise to God, do not delay in following through, for God takes no pleasure in fools. Keep all the promises you make to him. It is better to say nothing than to make a promise and not keep it."**
>
> ECCLESIASTES 5:4-5

In addition to maintaining the integrity of one's word, Christians should also obey the word of God because doing otherwise means one is a liar, the Bible says the truth is not in such a person.

> **"And this is how we know [daily, by experience] that we have come to know Him [to understand Him and be more deeply acquainted with Him]: if we *habitually* keep [focused on His precepts and obey] His commandments (teachings). Whoever says, "I have come to know Him," but does not *habitually* keep [focused on His precepts and obey] His commandments (teachings), is a liar, and the truth [of the divine word] is not in him."**
>
> 1 JOHN 2:3-4

PRAYER

Dear Lord Jesus, we pray for the grace to be honest, trustworthy, and truthful, so that our words are not held against us in Jesus' name. Amen.

CHAPTER 45

Listen to Godly Advice

> "A wise child accepts a parent's discipline; a mocker refuses to listen to correction."
>
> PROVERBS 13:1

The wisdom nugget is for children and young people to listen to the godly instruction, counsel, advice and guidance of parents or godly people in authority over them. Whenever children listen to and obey godly counsel, their lives turn out great, they become great adults in the future. They contribute positively to society and gladden their parents' and guardians' hearts by making them proud of their great achievements and contribution to the world.

> "Sensible children bring joy to their father; foolish children despise their mother."
>
> PROVERBS 15:20

> "The father of a righteous man will greatly rejoice, and he who fathers a wise son will delight in him."
>
> PROVERBS 23:24

> "A man who loves wisdom brings joy to his father, but a companion of prostitutes squanders his wealth."
>
> PROVERBS 29:3

However, it must be emphasised that parents ought to teach and correct their children with love and never provoke or abuse them. Parents must show their children the right way of living, teaching them the word of God and never taking advantage of their youth but helping them do life well in a righteous manner.

> "Fathers, do not provoke your children to anger [do not exasperate them to the point of resentment with demands that are trivial or unreasonable or humiliating or abusive; nor by showing favouritism or indifference to any of them], but bring them up [tenderly, with lovingkindness] in the discipline and instruction of the Lord."
>
> EPHESIANS 6:4

The lesson is for children to have a sound judgement and to listen to good advice and corrections and for parents to teach their children the way of the Lord so they can live righteously.

PRAYER

Let us pray for every child and young person that God will give them sound judgement and the grace to listen to advice in Jesus' name. Amen.

CHAPTER 46

Parental Discipline

> "He who withholds the rod [of discipline] hates his son, but he who loves him disciplines and trains him diligently and appropriately [with wisdom and love]."
>
> PROVERBS 13:24

The first thing to clarify is that this scripture is not demanding parents to result in physical abuse to correct their children. Training with the rod simply means disciplining them by informing them and teaching them the ways of God. The wisdom nugget is, therefore, to correct children with love and not violence, speaking positive, edifying and godly words of affirmation, to build up and not tear down their character.

The intention and common goal of discipline should be to develop children and young people into great members of society. Discipline is, therefore, the practice of training young people and teaching them the act of obedience. The aim should be to help them learn to obey godly instructions and the code of conduct for good behaviour. The style used should not be abusive or become a cover to maltreat children.

Discipline is a godly duty for parents, a refusal to correct one's children is neglect of parental duties of love. A notable example of a father that disciplines his children is God Almighty himself as previously discussed in previous chapters. The Bible says God, disciplines his people as their Father because he loves them and wants them to do well in life. The Bible says those whom God loves he disciplines to develop them into godly people.

> "For the LORD corrects those he loves, just as a father corrects a child in whom he delights."
>
> PROVERBS 3:12

Children should treat discipline as an instrument of love for development. The Bible teaches young people to endure any suffering that is associated with godly discipline. Discipline has the reward of producing great young adults for glorious living. It cultivates self-discipline, self-control, love, and the fear of God in young people.

God appreciates fathers who discipline and command their household, he praised and selected Abraham and made him the father of nations because of his ability to discipline and command his children and household to a godly lifestyle.

> "As for Me, behold, my covenant is with you, and [as a result] you shall be the father of many nations. "No longer shall your name be Abram (exalted father), But your name shall be Abraham (father of a multitude); For I will make you the father of many nations."
>
> GENESIS 17:4-5

> "For I have chosen him so that he will command his children and his house after him to keep the way of the LORD by doing what is right and just. This is how the LORD will fulfil to Abraham what he promised him."
>
> GENESIS 18:19

However, fathers should not provoke their children, by using excessive force or oppressive punishment in their parenting method. Discipline is a partnership between the greater and the lesser, the lesser cheerfully obeys the greater and follows their godly corrections and teachings.

The use of physical violence or verbal abuse must not be a means of correcting children because that will become child abuse, a crime punishable by law. Discipline should be a verbal correction, a written instruction, or a withholding of certain benefits from the child to help them reflect on their behaviour.

Proverbs focuses more on the discipleship of young people. It is the responsibility of parents and guardians to train their children by setting a series of godly rules for them to follow. There are retributions whenever a Believer or a child disobeys such orders to dissuade them from becoming hardened sinners or wayward children.

God's law, in the Ten Commandment, promises the reward of long life to those who respect, honour, and obey their parents' discipline. This promise is still very much alive because Apostle Paul reiterated the law in his letter to the Ephesians in the New Testament Bible.

> **"Honour your father and mother." This is the first commandment with a promise: If you honour your father and mother, "things will go well for you, and you will have a long life on the earth."**
>
> EPHESIANS 6:2-3

PRAYER

Dear Lord, we pray for parents all over the world, that they will have the wisdom and courage to discipline their children with love in Jesus' name. Amen.

CHAPTER 47

Wisdom and Building a Successful Home

> "The wise woman builds her house [on a foundation of godly precepts, and her household thrives], But the foolish one [who lacks spiritual insight] tears it down with her own hands [by ignoring godly principles]."
>
> PROVERBS 14:1

The wisdom nugget is to be wise and implement godly principles in the affairs of the home. This Bible passage encourages women particularly to be home builders who deploy godly ideas in running their household and family affairs. It takes wisdom to run a successful home because coordinating people of different characters, personalities, and needs, will require wisdom.

The person who runs the home makes a wise decision to build a successful home, based upon the solid foundation of God's word and commandment, which is love. The Bible says a house is built upon wisdom and established by understanding (Proverbs 24:3). Therefore, building a home requires determination and the ability to focus on the bigger picture of things. It requires asking the question; what is the greater good for all members of the family?

It demands selflessness, love, patience, long-suffering, and sacrifice with the will to compromise, and remain calm whenever there are disagreements between members of the family. Proverbs 12:16 says members of the family should be emotionally mature and be able to shrug off insults to avoid unnecessary angry outbursts or quarrels which can tear down the home and destroy the peace and unity of the home.

Fools do not follow this godly instruction to build a successful home, instead, they, destroy their home by allowing unnecessary quarrels to develop into resentments, bitterness and eventually separation or even divorce in marriages. Running a household, whether by a female or male head, therefore, requires all members of the family, to share common goals, visions, values, and direction.

That way, everyone knows the important values to abide by daily as members of the household to live together in peace and harmony. The Bible reiterate that no two people can walk together except if they agree with one another. This means family members cannot live peacefully with one another unless they walk in unity and agreement.

> **"Can two people walk together without agreeing on the direction?"**
>
> AMOS 3:3

It takes love and patience to build a home, the Bible says love covers a multitude of sins and gives people the grace to forgive each other and the will to show kindness, compassion, and mercy. The divine way to build a peaceful and happy home is therefore by the help of the Holy Spirit. The fruit of the Holy Spirit, love, joy, peace, longsuffering, goodness, patience, and generosity all contribute to the success of a godly home.

The Way of Love – The Fruit of the Holy Spirit

> "But the fruit of the Spirit [the result of His presence within us] is love [unselfish concern for others], joy, [inner] peace, patience [not the ability to wait, but how we act while waiting], kindness, goodness, faithfulness, gentleness, self-control. Against such things, there is no law."
>
> GALATIANS 5:22-23

Where there is love, there will be peace and family members will live together in harmony. The Bible promises God's command of blessing upon the people who dwell in unity.

God's Blessing Upon the Family that Live in Unity

> "A song of ascents. Of David. How good and pleasant it is when God's people live together in unity! It is like precious oil poured on the head, running down on the beard, running down on Aaron's beard, down on the collar of his robe. It is as if the dew of Hermon were falling on Mount Zion. For there the LORD bestows his blessing, even life forevermore."
>
> PSALM 133:1-3

PRAYER

Glorious Father, we thank you for homes all over the world, we ask for the grace to love one another and to build our homes on the foundation of Christ, living peacefully and in unity in Jesus' name. Amen.

CHAPTER 48

Be An Instrument of Peace - A Gentle Answer Diffuses Anger

> "A soft and gentle and thoughtful answer turns away wrath, but harsh and painful and careless words stir up anger."
>
> PROVERBS 15:1

The wisdom nugget is to pursue peace and always speak gentle and calming words, especially to an angry person to avoid escalating their anger. A failure to do so usually results in quarrels, fights, or death in certain cases. There are situations where extreme rage has escalated to manslaughter or murder. So, the best way is to negotiate peacefully with others.

We have road rage incidents where an angry driver runs over a fellow road user during an outburst of anger and rage. Furthermore, there are crime stories of domestic violence or fights in communities escalating to manslaughter or murder, where an angry person intentionally or accidentally kills the other person in a rage.

A good biblical story that illustrates the need to do life with thoughtful answers or responses to anger is the encounter between Nabal and David.

In 1 Samuel 25, David politely requested a favour from Nabal to give some provision to him and his men, who had faithfully cared for his sheep and ensured no harm came to his servants whilst in the desert, but the man reacted angrily and replied with disdain.

David became angry and planned to kill Nabal and his family members. Abigail, Nabal's wife who later became David's wife, interceded for her household, appealing to David to let God avenge him over her foolish husband. She spoke nice and calming words, saying her husband acted like a fool because his name meant a fool.

Abigail's gentle words calmed David and won his heart, he relented in his anger and spared the lives of Nabal's household even though Nabal suddenly dropped dead later in the story. God took revenge for David and killed Nabal for his austere and meanness of soul. So, David got the reward of Abigail as his wife.

Nabal's Foolish Words

"Who is this fellow, David?" Nabal sneered at the young men. "Who does this son of Jesse think he is? There are lots of servants these days who run away from their masters. Should I take my bread and my water and the meat that I've slaughtered for my shearers and give it to a band of outlaws who come from who knows where?"

1 SAMUEL 25:10-11

David's Anger

"Now David had said, "Surely in vain I have protected *and* guarded all that this man has in the wilderness so that nothing was missing of all that belonged to him, and he has repaid me evil for good. May God do so to the enemies of David, and more also, if by morning I leave [alive] even one male of any who belongs to him."

1 SAMUEL 25:21-22

Abigail's Intercession and Calming Words

"When Abigail saw David, she hurried and dismounted from the donkey, and kneeled face downward before David and bowed down to the ground [in respect]. Kneeling at his feet she said, "My lord, let the blame *and* guilt be on me alone. And please let your maidservant speak to you and listen to the words of your maidservant. Please do not let my lord pay attention to this worthless man, Nabal, for as his name is, so is he. Nabal (fool) is his name and foolishness (stupidity) is with him, but I your maidservant did not see my lord's young men whom you sent. So now, my lord, as the LORD lives, and as your soul lives, since the LORD has prevented you from shedding blood, and from avenging yourself by your hand, now then let your enemies and those who seek to do evil to my lord, be as [self-destructive as] Nabal. Now this gift, which your maidservant has brought my lord, let it be given to the young men who accompany *and* follow my lord. Please forgive the transgression of your maidservant; for the LORD will certainly make my lord a secure *and* enduring house, because my lord is fighting the battles of the LORD, and evil will not be found in you all your days. Should anyone rise to pursue you and to seek your life, then the life of my lord will be bound in the [precious] bundle of the living with the LORD your God; but the lives of your enemies—those He will hurl out as from the centre of a sling. And it will happen when the LORD does for my lord according to all the good that He has spoken (promised) concerning you and appoints you ruler over Israel that this [incident] will not cause grief or [bring] a troubled conscience to my lord, both by having shed blood without cause and by my lord having avenged himself.

When the LORD deals well with my lord, then remember [with favour] your maidservant." ."

1 SAMUEL 25:23-31

Abigail's thoughtful words diffuse David's anger

David said to Abigail, "Blessed be the LORD, the God of Israel, who sent you to meet me this day. And blessed be your discretion *and* discernment, and blessed be you, who has kept me from bloodshed this day and from avenging myself by my hand. Nevertheless, as the LORD the God of Israel lives, who has prevented me from harming you, if you had not come quickly to meet me, most certainly by the morning light there would not have been left to Nabal so much as one male. So, David accepted what she had brought to him and said to her, "Go up to your house in peace. See, I have listened to you and have granted your request."

1 SAMUEL 25:32-35

Notice Nabal spoke rashly but his wife Abigail spoke gentle words and brought peace to the situation. Her calming words diffused David's anger and brought peace to her family. The great lesson from Nabal's story is not to be a fool whilst facing an angry situation. Retaliation or angry words will only escalate the situation rather than diffuse it. Meanwhile, a soft and gentle answer will calm the situation and maintain peace.

"A hot-tempered man stirs up strife, but he who is slow to anger calms a dispute."

PROVERBS 15:18

"Through patience, a ruler can be persuaded, and a gentle tongue can break a bone."

PROVERBS 25:15

PRAYER

Lord, we pray for the grace to be patient. We ask for the wisdom to speak gentle words when dealing with an angry situation in Jesus' name. Amen.

CHAPTER 49

Genuine Prayers Triumphs Hypocrisy

> "The sacrifice of the wicked is hateful and exceedingly offensive to the LORD, But the prayer of the upright is His delight!"
>
> PROVERBS 15:8

The Bible says God detest fake people who show off their hypocrisy. The wisdom nugget of this scripture is to be sincere and humble, especially during prayer. Prayer is not an egocentric self-centred act that a person can use to show off their piety or self-importance. Prayer should be a genuine communication with God, offered in sincerity and humility. Jesus gave the format for prayer in the Book of Matthew.

> "But when you pray, go into your most private room, close the door, and pray to your Father who is in secret. And when you pray, do not use meaningless repetition as the Gentiles do, for they think they will be heard because of their many words, and your Father who sees [what is done] in secret will reward you."
>
> MATTHEW 6:6-7

Jesus gave a good illustration of what not to do in prayer in the parable of the Pharisee and the Taxman in Luke chapter 18.

> "Two men went to the Temple to pray. One was a Pharisee, and the other was a despised tax collector. The Pharisee stood by himself and prayed this prayer: 'I thank you, God, that I am not like other people—cheaters, sinners, adulterers. I am certainly not like that tax collector! I fast twice a week, and I give you a tenth of my income.'
>
> "But the tax collector stood at a distance and dared not even lift his eyes to heaven as he prayed. Instead, he beat his chest in sorrow, saying, 'O God, be merciful to me, for I am a sinner.'
>
> I tell you, this sinner, not the Pharisee, returned home justified before God. For those who exalt themselves will be humbled, and those who humble themselves will be exalted."
>
> LUKE 18:10-14

So, Jesus' advice is for Believers not to be hypocritical in places of prayer but to conduct prayer with dignity, humility, sincerity, and integrity without arrogance or pomposity.

PRAYER

Dear Lord Jesus, we ask that you help us keep a humble prayer life in Jesus' name. Amen.

CHAPTER 50

Optimism, Hope, Joy, and a Cheerful Heart

> "A heart full of joy and goodness makes a cheerful face, but when a heart is full of sadness the spirit is crushed."
>
> PROVERBS 15:13

The wisdom nugget in this scripture is to be cheerful and have an optimistic view of life. Christians should be merry and happy because a happy person inspires others to happiness. Cheerfulness means having a smile on one's face and being hopeful. Hope helps the Believer trust in God with an optimistic view that all will be well as they hope for the best.

The world is full of problems and there are always reasons to be sad, unhappy, and depressed in life, but the Bible promises God's people overflowing joy, a joy that flows and rubs off others. Joy is a fruit of the spirit, given by the presence of the Holy Spirit. It is a state of blessedness found in trusting God which gives the Believer hope for a bright future. On the other hand, those who lack faith often hold a pessimistic view of life and remain miserable people without hope for a bright future.

Hope that all will be well is a form of faith that Believers have in times of trouble or challenges in life, so they go through life believing in the big

God who has them in the palm of his hands. God is Jehovah Jireh, Jehovah Nissi and El Shaddai so he protects and provides for his people. A knowledge of who God is and knowing that he will care and do his best for his people, keeps the Believer focused on the bigger picture of life, with the hope that all will be well with them.

The Bible declares the just shall live by faith! Living by faith helps the Believer live a happy and prosperous life. Cheerfulness has a health benefit; the Bible says it is like medicine for the heart which makes a person strong and healthy because happiness gives strength whereas sadness brings misery. Most importantly, the cheerful live a joyful life in a celebrative mood regardless of their circumstances in life.

> **"And Nehemiah continued, "Go and celebrate with a feast of rich foods and sweet drinks and share gifts of food with people who have nothing prepared. This is a sacred day before our Lord. Do not be dejected and sad, for the joy of the LORD is your strength!"**
>
> NEHEMIAH 8:10

> **"A happy heart is a good medicine, *and* a joyful mind causes healing, but a broken spirit dries up the bones."**
>
> PROVERBS 17:22

> **"All the days of the afflicted are bad, but a glad heart has a continual feast [regardless of the circumstances]."**
>
> PROVERBS 15:15

The Bible encourages the Believer to be cheerful and live life with a smile during adversity. A good illustration is the Bible story of the Shunammite woman, whose son died, yet when asked by Elisha's servant how she was, she responded, simply: "It is well!"

The Serenity of the Shunammite Woman

> "Please run now to meet her and ask her, 'Is it well with you? Is it well with your husband? Is it well with the child?'" And she answered, "It is well."
>
> 2 KINGS 4:26

Her optimism, calmness and faith helped her remain focused on God. She maintained her peace, calmness, hope, and joy in the face of adversity. She was a charitable woman who took care of the prophets of God, so, she got her son raised to life by Prophet Elisha.

The Bible promises the people of God peace and overflowing joy regardless of their circumstances. Apostle Paul prayed for Christians to have joy, which flows from the presence of God the Holy Spirit, so, cheerfulness spring forth from within the soul and Spirit, it cannot be obtained from the outer world or experiences of life. Such emotion is mere happiness, not the supernatural joy inspired by God the Holy Spirit.

> "I pray that God, the source of hope, will fill you with joy and peace because you trust in him. Then you will overflow with confident hope through the power of the Holy Spirit."
>
> ROMANS 15:13

From the preceding scripture, we learn that Joy is the source of cheerfulness. Joy is different from happiness which is an emotion that responds to a happy event, so, a person can easily become sad whenever their situation changes for the bad. On the other hand, joy and cheerfulness is a feeling of happiness that is inside a person with or without any pleasurable event.

Joy is the fruit of the Holy Spirit, a feeling of immense pleasure that the Believer feels just by having faith in Christ Jesus (Galatians 5:22). And it is with this fruit of joy, that Believers live cheerfully with hope, bringing overflowing joy to other people around them because the smile and joy of one person can rob off another and inspire joy in their broken life.

PRAYER

Lord Jesus, we pray for the fruit of the Holy Spirit, joy, to fill the people of God, so, we can radiate and overflow with joy and peace of the Holy Spirit in Jesus' name. Amen.

CHAPTER 51

Seek Good Counsel to Succeed

> *"Plans go wrong for lack of advice; many advisers bring success."*
>
> PROVERBS 15:22

This is self-explanatory, the wisdom nugget is to seek the counsel of those who are wise and the advice of people with insight to establish success. The Bible emphasise individuals and nations do well when they have good counsellors and great leadership.

> "Without wise leadership, a nation falls; there is safety in having many advisers."
>
> PROVERBS 11:14

On the other hand, where there is no intelligent guidance, the people fail, the lesson is to surround oneself with a range of intelligent people who have sound judgement. There are options on how to obtain good counsel. Advise could come freely from family and friends who have insight into specific areas of life. Advice could come from professionals who have insight and skill or from mentors and coaches who have expertise or skills in specific areas of life relevant to one's needs.

Whilst taking professional counsel may be at a cost, overall, it is usually worth the expense because mistakes made in certain aspects of life could be catastrophic to a person's finances. Counsellors, therefore, give the benefit of financial security, their good advice usually save money overall.

Professional advice protects and helps a person live in securely. Whenever, there is a need to protect one's security, particularly national security, the use of expert intelligence is always useful. Therefore, nations do intelligence gathering to help protect their citizens against wars and other insecurities.

God is a counsellor; his word provides Christians with wisdom for every situation. It is therefore wise to study the word of God for revelation and guidance in every circumstance of life. The Bible says Jesus Christ is a counsellor (Isaiah 9:6) and he asked the Father to give Believers another counsellor (the Holy Spirit) to replace him after he left the earth.

> **"But the Helper (Comforter, Advocate, Intercessor—Counsellor, Strengthener, Standby), the Holy Spirit, whom the Father will send in My name [in My place, to represent Me and act on My behalf], He will teach you all things. And He will help you remember everything that I have told you."**
>
> JOHN 14:26

PRAYER

Father in heaven, we thank you for the wisdom of your word and the guidance of the Holy Spirit. We pray that you surround us with divine counsellors in our journey of life in Jesus' name. Amen.

CHAPTER 52

Appropriate Answers and Timely Word

> "A man has joy in giving an appropriate answer, and how good and delightful is a word spoken at the right moment—how good it is!"
>
> PROVERBS 15:23

The wisdom nugget of this proverb is to speak the right words at the right moment. Such words are called words in season. They are spoken at the appropriate time to meet the need in a person's life. They bring solutions and resolutions to issues of life. Learning to speak timely words is refreshing to the human soul. The wisdom is to develop a wise tongue. Isaiah calls it, the learned tongue. And Apostle Paul calls it a tongue seasoned with salt.

> "The Lord GOD has given Me the tongue of the learned, that I should know how to speak a word in season to *him who is* weary. He awakens me morning by morning. He awakens my ear to hear as the learned."
>
> ISAIAH 50:4

> "Let your speech at all times be gracious *and* pleasant, seasoned with salt, so that you will know how to answer each one [who questions you]."
>
> COLOSSIANS 4:6

God help his people know what to say at the right moment. The Holy Spirit, the spirit of God in the Believer divinely speaks through the people of God. Moses at his call to leadership was reluctant to accept the job. He said he was a stammerer unable to speak properly, but the Lord encouraged him that he would teach him to speak. God also encouraged Jeremiah and put his words in his mouth.

> "Then the LORD asked Moses, "Who makes a person's mouth? Who decides whether people speak or do not speak, hear, or do not hear, see, or do not see? Is it not I, the LORD? Now, go! I will be with you as you speak, and I will instruct you in what to say."
>
> EXODUS 4:11-12

> "Then the LORD reached out and touched my mouth and said, "Look, I have put my words in your mouth!"
>
> JEREMIAH 1:9

The Holy Spirit help the Believer in their response to people so that they speak with wisdom, especially to their opponents or adversaries.

> "And when you are brought to trial in the synagogues and before rulers and authorities, don't worry about how to defend yourself or what to say, for the Holy Spirit will teach you at that time what needs to be said."
>
> LUKE 12:11-12

> "For I will give you the right words and such wisdom that none of your opponents will be able to reply or refute you!"
>
> LUKE 21:15

> "For it is not you who will be speaking—it will be the Spirit of your Father speaking through you."
>
> MATTHEW 10:20

Whenever a person speaks with the help of the Holy Spirit, others marvel. A notable example is the teaching of the Lord Jesus, whenever, he taught the word of God with in-depth understanding and the people asked questions, about how he got such wisdom and insight.

> **"Everyone spoke well of him and was amazed by the gracious words that came from his lips. "How can this be?" they asked. "Isn't this Joseph's son?"**
>
> LUKE 4:22

> **"Then, midway through the festival, Jesus went up to the Temple and began to teach. The people were surprised when they heard him. "How does he know so much when he hasn't been trained?" they asked."**
>
> JOHN 7:14-15

Christians can pray and ask for the grace of anointed lips that speak words of blessings at the appropriate seasons.

> **"You are the most excellent of men and your lips have been anointed with grace since God has blessed you forever."**
>
> PSALM 45:2

PRAYER

Dear Lord, we ask for the wisdom to speak words in season in Jesus' name. Amen.

CHAPTER 53

Peace With Enemies

> "When a man's ways please the LORD, He makes even his enemies be at peace with him."
>
> PROVERBS 16:7

The wisdom nugget is to focus on pleasing God and live according to his will. God elevates godly people, making them shine brightly so enemies reckon with them and recognise the grace of God upon them. He is delighted with those whose ways please him; he makes them objects of compassion and favour.

> **"He caused all who held them captive to show them mercy."**
>
> PSALM 106: 46

A good illustration is the Bible story of Jacob and his brother. Jacob cheated the brother of his firstborn birthright and robbed him of the blessing of their father. With their mother's help, Jacob fled to his maternal uncle, Laban's house to avoid death by Esau.

> **"From that time on, Esau hated Jacob because their father had given Jacob the blessing. And Esau began to scheme: "I**

will soon be mourning my father's death. Then I will kill my brother, Jacob."

> GENESIS 27:41

God approved Jacob because he was a righteous man, his brother Esau, who became his enemy, welcomed him, and relented on his intention to take revenge when Jacob returned to Israel several years later.

> "Then Esau ran to meet him and embraced him, threw his arms around his neck, and kissed him. And they both wept."
>
> GENESIS 33:4

Apostle Paul's words in the Book of Romans nicely wrapped up this wisdom. He cited, that if God is for the Believer, no enemy can stand against them.

> "What then shall we say to all these things? If God is for us, who can be [successful] against us?"
>
> ROMANS 8:31

Moreover, the Bible says God will go the extra mile in granting his people so much favour that their enemies will bless them with gifts. This happened when the Israelites departed Egypt, the Egyptians freely gave them their gold and silver.

> "And I will grant this people favour *and* respect in the sight of the Egyptians; therefore, it shall be that when you go, you will not go empty-handed."
>
> EXODUS 3:21

"And the people of Israel did as Moses had instructed; they asked the Egyptians for clothing and articles of silver and gold. The LORD caused the Egyptians to look favourably on the

Israelites, and they gave the Israelites whatever they asked for. So, they stripped the Egyptians of their wealth!"

EXODUS 12:35-36

PRAYER

Dear Lord, we give you thanks for your love for your people. We pray for the grace to do life in a manner that is pleasing to you, so, that we can live peacefully, even with our enemies in Jesus' name. Amen.

CHAPTER 54

Commit Your Plans to God

> "A man's mind plans his way [as he journeys through life],
> But the LORD directs his steps and establishes them."
>
> PROVERBS 37:23

The wisdom nugget is to commit one's plans to God because he alone has the final say in human destinies and purposes. An adage says man proposes but God disposes of. Simply put, one may make plans of how to live but it is only by God's grace that human plans are possible.

God is the creator and giver of life to every human being. Therefore, Christians ought to commit their lives and ways to God for safekeeping and direction. The Bible says God will help his people accomplish their goals in life.

> "Commit everything you do to the LORD. Trust him, and he will help you."
>
> PSALM 37:5

> "Commit to the LORD whatever you do, and he will establish your plans."
>
> PROVERBS 16:3

God loves his people and his thoughts towards them are thoughts of good and peace, and he wants them to achieve their purpose and get to their expected end in life (Jeremiah 29:11-13). The Bible confirms God's thoughts are not simply good but great. No one can imagine how great and wonderful God's intentions are towards the people who love him.

> **"However, as it is written: "What no eye has seen, what no ear has heard, and what no human mind has conceived" — the things God has prepared for those who love him."**
>
> 1 CORINTHIANS 2:9

So, if God loves his people, and has a plan that is so grandeur, which is beyond human imagination according to the Bible, why then, should the Believer lay out their plans and different agendas? Will it not be wiser to seek God's will and plan, so that, life can be a celebration rather than a pain. Disappointment, frustration, and inferior quality of life with bad effects follow those who disregard God's purpose for their life.

There was a man in the Bible, called the Rich Fool, because he based his business plans on his thoughts, plans and agenda without seeking or acknowledging God. In the Parable, Jesus told how the man's land yielded abundant harvest, so he said to himself, what shall I do? I have no place to store my crops, good thought, one would think! But then, he further said, I will tear down my barns and build a bigger one and store my surplus grain and say to myself, you have sufficient grain laid up for years, so take life easy, eat, drink and be merry.

But God said to him, you fool! This very night, your life will be demanded of you. Then who will get what you have prepared for yourself? This is how it will be with whoever stores up things for themselves but is not rich towards God (Luke12:16-21).

James clarified this matter further in the book of James, he wrote what we can take as a good guideline as Christians when making plans.

> "Yet you do not know [the least thing] about what may happen in your life tomorrow. [What is secure in your life?] You are *merely* a vapour [like a puff of smoke or a wisp of steam from a cooking pot] that is visible for a little while and then vanishes [into thin air]. Come now [and pay attention to this], you who say, "Today or tomorrow we will go to such and such a city and spend a year there and carry on our business and make a profit. Instead, you ought to say, "If the Lord wills, we will live and we will do this or that."
>
> JAMES 4:13-15

The lesson to draw from this scripture is to seek God for his divine will, before making any long-term plans about how or what to do with one's time, investment, ambitions, dreams, vision, and other life goals. One must learn not to boast about tomorrow and to pay attention to God's will and plans because only those will prevail.

> "Many are the plans in a person's heart, but it is the LORD's purpose that prevails."
>
> PROVERBS 19:21

> "Don't brag about tomorrow, since you don't know what the day will bring."
>
> PROVERBS 27:1

PRAYER

Dear Lord, we thank you for your love and guidance, we pray, that you guide every Christian in their daily work and plans in Jesus' name. Amen.

CHAPTER 55

Do Not Gloat Over Misfortune

> "Those who mock the poor, insult their Maker; those who rejoice at the misfortune of others will be punished."
>
> PROVERBS 17:5

The wisdom nugget of Proverbs 17:5 is not to gloat over other people's disasters, however, tempting that might be. Especially when it is of their own making; "I told you so" is a phrase, so, tempting when things go wrong, for those who fail to heed warnings or advice.

The wisdom for doing life successfully is never to rejoice when others fail or fall. The Bible says when the righteous fall, he will rise again. So, never rejoice over another's calamities of life because God will punish anyone who does.

> "The godly may trip seven times, but they will get up again. But one disaster is enough to overthrow the wicked."
>
> PROVERBS 24:16

> "Many are the afflictions of the righteous, but the LORD delivers him from them all."
>
> PSALM 34:19

> "Though he falls, he will not be overwhelmed, for the LORD is holding his hand."
>
> PSALM 37:24
> PROVERBS 24:17

> "Don't rejoice when your enemies fall; don't be happy when they stumble."
>
> OBADIAH 1:12

> "Do not rejoice over me [amid my tragedies], O my enemy! Though I fall, I will rise; Though I sit in the darkness [of distress], the LORD is a light for me."
>
> MICAH 7:8

The beginning part of Proverbs 17:5 teaches God's people not to mock poor people because they are God's creation. Christians should bless the poor in whatever way they can.

PRAYER

Dear Lord, we pray, that you help us not to be mockers of the poor. We ask for the grace never to gloat over other people's misfortunes in Jesus' name. Amen.

CHAPTER 56
Loyalty in Relationships

> "A friend is always loyal, and a brother is born to help in time of need."
>
> PROVERBS 17:17

This proverb defines the key requirements of friendship and family relationships as faithfulness, love, and loyalty. Friends should remain loyal to each other, and family members should be available, whenever possible, to help each other. Christians ought to be kind and relentless in their relationships. The wisdom nugget is to be loving, loyal, faithful, steadfast, and merciful in relationships. The godly foundation of relationships is love.

God desires his people to love one another. Therefore, friends and family members ought to love one another and show each other compassion and loving devotion. When one is in trouble or cries, the other should be there to support, encourage and ease their pains (a trouble shared is a trouble halved). They should also be generous and rejoice with one another, celebrating each other's life wins, being each other's cheerleader and companion through life's challenges and victories.

> "I am giving you a new commandment, that you love one another. Just as I have loved you, so you too are to love one another."
>
> JOHN 13:34

However, unreliable friends and family members betray and destroy each other. Whilst a person cannot choose their family members, they can at least choose their friends. The Bible, therefore, advises the Believer to choose their friends carefully.

> "The man of *too many* friends [chosen indiscriminately] will be broken in pieces *and* come to ruin, but there is a [true, loving] friend who [is reliable and] sticks closer than a brother."
>
> PROVERBS 18:24

There was a woman in the Book of Ruth, who showed the people of God, how to be loyal members of the family. Ruth, a young wife whose father-in-law and her husband died, decided to return with her mother-in-law to her homeland Israel. Naomi her mother-in-law and her late husband had fled to Moab, to avoid the famine in Israel.

Naomi told Ruth to stay in her country, Moab, but she refused. She followed Naomi, saying wherever she goes to live, she will follow, worship her God, and die. She portrayed the stickability unto death expected from family members as stated in Proverbs 17:17.

Ruth's Loyalty to Naomi

> "But Ruth replied, "Do not ask me to leave you and turn back. Wherever you go, I will go; wherever you live, I will live. Your people will be my people, and your God will be my God, wherever you die, I will die, and there, I will be buried. May the LORD punish me severely if I allow anything but death to separate us!"
>
> RUTH 1:16

The friendship between Jonathan and David portrays the faithfulness required in the relationship between friends. Jonathan had no complaints about David taking the throne, even though, he was the heir to the throne as King Saul's son (1 Samuel 18). There was also great solidarity between David and his soldiers, they were willing to defend and follow his leadership until death. When he asked an official to return from following him when he fled from his son Absalom who overthrew his kingship, the man refused to go back.

> **"You arrived only recently, and should I force you today to wander with us? I don't even know where we will go. Go on back and take your kinsmen with you, and may the LORD show you his unfailing love and faithfulness. But, Ittai said to the king, "I vow by the LORD and by your own life that I will go wherever my lord the king goes, no matter what happens—whether it means life or death."**
>
> 2 SAMUEL 15:20-21

David was quite impressed with his loyalty that he prayed for him for God to show him loving-kindness. Such loyalty and devotion usually bring blessing to whoever practises loyalty as a principle in love and friendship. God is loyal and faithful to his people too.

PRAYER

Almighty Father, we ask for discerning spirit and the wisdom to select great friends to do life with. Help us to have the unfailing love and loyalty required to maintain great relationships in Jesus' name. Amen.

CHAPTER 57

There is Power and Protection in God's Names

> *"The name of the LORD is a strong tower; the righteous runs to it and is safe and set on high [far above evil]."*
>
> PROVERBS 18:10

The wisdom nugget is to look onto the divine names of God for security and safety. The Lord is a fortress to his people, he is a place of strength and power, where they can hide from the dangers of life and navigate life safely from the evil one and his tricks.

The Bible says God has given Jesus a name above every other name, so, every situation and the issue of life, must bow at the mention of his name. There is protection for the people of God in the names of God Almighty and the name of his son Jesus Christ, the saviour.

> "Therefore, God elevated him to the place of highest honour and gave him the name above all other names, that at the name of Jesus every knee should bow, in heaven and on earth and under the earth, and every tongue declare that Jesus Christ is Lord, to the glory of God the Father."
>
> PHILIPPIANS 2:9-11

There is power in the name of Jesus, he protects the people of God with his name, so, in the name of Jesus, every Believer is safe from the devil.

> **"During my time here, I protected them by the power of the name you gave me. I guarded them so that no one was lost, except the one headed for destruction, as the Scriptures foretold."**
>
> JOHN 17:12

PRAYER

Mighty God, we thank you for your name exalted above all names in which the Believer can find power, protection, strength, and safety. We pray that you protect every Christian from the evil one in the mighty name of Jesus. Amen.

CHAPTER 58

The Act of Listening Before Speaking

> "He who answers before he hears [the facts]—
> It is folly and shame to him."
>
> PROVERBS 18:13

The wisdom nugget is to hear the facts first before deciding what to say. The Bible says to be swift to hear and slow to speak (James 1:19). This teaches the Believer to be patient in handling matters and to examine all avenues of the argument carefully before deciding on the best answer to give to opponents.

The lesson is to diligently explore all answers and solutions before speaking or offering an opinion. This is like the world's unwritten 24-hour rule of the decision-making process which advises 24 hours to think a matter through and reflect properly before speaking or taking important decisions. A sleepover on thoughts and ideas usually helps a person make clearer and wiser decisions.

> **"Then you must inquire, probe, and investigate it thoroughly. And if it is true and it has been proved that this detestable thing has been done among you."**
>
> DEUTERONOMY 13:14

The Bible illustrated this further with how decisions are made in the court of law. Arguments from both parties are presented to the court before the judge can offer the judgement or the jury can arrive at a decision in the case at hand.

> **"Does our Law convict someone without first giving him a hearing and finding out what he is [accused of] doing?"**
>
> JOHN 7:51

PRAYER

Dear Lord, our Messiah the anointed one, we ask for the patience and the grace to listen before we speak in Jesus' name. Amen.

CHAPTER 59

The Power of Motivation and a Healthy Spirit

> "The human spirit can endure a sick body, but who can bear a crushed spirit?"
>
> PROVERBS 18:14

The wisdom nugget is to keep a cheerful spirit and avoid having a broken or a grieved spirit. The negative emotion from a broken spirit leads to hopelessness, discouragement, and despair. The repercussion is the destruction of the person with the crushed spirit.

To understand the truth of Proverbs 18:14, it is necessary to give a description or meaning of the Spirit. There are two meanings or approaches to defining the spirit. First, human beings, are composed of body, soul, and spirit. The spirit is the centre, the non-physical part of a person, and the soul is the seat of emotions and character. The spirit is the inner self and the inner being, the divine nature of a person that never dies.

On the other hand, the spirit is the prevailing mood or attitude of a person. The motivating force that propels a person, is the seat of faith, hope and confidence. This second meaning is what the Bible is referring to in

Proverbs 18:14. Without the motivation to survive or the willpower to live, people have been known to die of hopelessness.

People who have terminal illnesses have been known to survive with hope and determination. Meanwhile, those burdened with lesser challenges of life but who have no willpower fail because of their broken spirit. Sometimes when such people fall ill, they simply give in to the sickness and die without fighting for their lives.

The lesson is to adopt a posture of faith and to be positive in every situation to prevent discouragement, sadness, and a crushed spirit. Apostle Paul taught his disciple, Timothy to fight the good fight of faith (1 Timothy 6:11) and to keep his spirit up with his faith in God, knowing with God all things are possible.

From the standpoint of faith in Christ Jesus, Christians are overcomers; in all circumstances, they are more than conquerors. In addition to faith, the Bible says a merry and cheerful heart will cure depression and bring a person hope because according to Nehemiah, joy gives strength (Nehemiah 8:10) and Proverbs says it is like medicine for healing the mind (Proverbs 17:22).

There is good news for anyone with a broken heart, there is comfort and healing in Christ Jesus. Prophet Jeremiah asks the question; is there no balm in Gilead? Jesus is the balm for the healing of those with a broken spirit or depression. Jesus heals and binds the broken hearted, he gives his people, love, power, and a sound mind. He removes fear and heals those with sadness or depression.

> **"Is there no balm in Gilead? Is there no physician there? Why then is there no healing for the wound of my people?"**
>
> JEREMIAH 8:22

"He heals the broken-hearted and binds up their wounds [healing their pain and comforting their sorrow]."

PSALM 147:3

PRAYER

Father, we thank you for a spirit of love and power, we ask for healing for those with a broken spirit in Jesus' name. Amen.

CHAPTER 60

The Power of Gifts

> *"Giving a gift can open doors; it gives access to important people."*
>
> PROVERBS 18:16

The wisdom nugget is that gifts are an effective way of getting through doors of opportunities. A gift affects the emotions of the receiver positively thereby making them happy. Gifts bring a smile to the face of the receiver; they can pacify anger or get the attention of great people. Gifts delight the soul! The Bible likens the feelings felt when receiving gifts to that of when a person receives a rare gemstone.

However, gifts can influence the decision-making process causing the receiver to become biased or partial towards the giver. Hence, people give gifts as a bribe to curry favour or make friends especially with influential people. A Gift is therefore a useful tool that helps the giver prosper and succeed.

> *"A present is a precious stone in the eyes of its possessor; Wherever he turns, he prospers."*
>
> PROVERBS 17:8

> "Many seek favours from a ruler; everyone is the friend of a person who gives gifts!"
>
> PROVERBS 19:6

A gift is useful for pacifying anger or getting people's acceptance. Jacob sent gifts before him to help calm his brother Esau's anger to avoid his revenge against him.

> "A secret gift calms anger: a bribe under the table pacifies fury."
>
> PROVERBS 21:14

> "And so, Jacob commanded the second and the third as well, and all that followed the herds, saying, "This is what you shall say to Esau when you meet him; and you shall say, 'Look, your servant Jacob is behind us.'" For he said [to himself], "I will try to appease him with the gift that is going ahead of me. Then afterwards I will see him; perhaps he will accept *and* forgive me."
>
> GENESIS 32:19-20

An alternative interpretation of gift is talent or skill. It is often said that a person's talent or skill can bring them before great men. This means people's talents and skillsets can get them highly paid positions of work.

> "A man's gift makes room for him and brings him before great men."
>
> PROVERBS 18:16

A splendid example is the Bible story of Joseph's rise to power in Egypt because of his gift of interpretation of dreams. He came before King Pharoah of Egypt to interpret the king's dreams, and from there, the king favoured him and made him the governor of Egypt with the power to manage the economy of Egypt even though he was a foreigner and a slave in the land (Genesis 41).

PRAYER

Lord Jesus, you are the gift of God to the world, we pray for the grace to be generous people and to know how to use our gifts and talent to win the favours of great people in Jesus' name. Amen.

CHAPTER 61
Marriage and Finding a Good Spouse

> "He who finds a [true and faithful] wife finds a good thing and obtains favour and approval from the LORD."
>
> PROVERBS 18:22

The wisdom nugget is finding a godly spouse is a blessing of the Lord. A good spouse is rare, so, finding such a person requires the favour of God. The biblical role of a wife is that of a helper, so, when God created man, he said, he will need a companion. Therefore, God created the woman, so, both his male and the female creations can live together and support each other throughout their lifetime. Finding a good relationship and companionship is, therefore, a blessing of God.

> "Now the LORD God said, "It is not good (beneficial) for the man to be alone; I will make him a helper [one who balances him—a counterpart who is] suitable *and* complementary for him."
>
> GENESIS 2:18

If God the creator acknowledges the need for a man not to be alone, Christians ought to consider marriage as an effective way to do life. Therefore, at a ripe age, a man should seek his God-given partner and ask for her hand in marriage. Being alone can create emotional problems such as loneliness which can, in turn, cause all sorts of negative effects on human beings such as depression and lack of motivation, progress, success, and happiness.

The Bible emphasised the power of two people working together. Whilst one can chase a thousand, two has the capacity of chasing ten thousand. What an exponential growth in the ability of two to achieve greater heights!

> **"How could one person chase a thousand of them, and two people put ten thousand to flight unless their Rock had sold them unless the LORD had given them up?"**
>
> DEUTERONOMY 32:30

Companionship makes life bearable and easier than when one lives alone. The Bible says two people are better than one because they can help and support each other and share the load and burdens of life. When one falls the other can help him up. And there is the benefit of keeping each other warm.

> **"Two people are better off than one, for they can help each other succeed. If one person falls, the other can reach out and help. But someone who falls alone is in real trouble. Likewise, two people lying close together can keep each other warm. But how can one be warm alone?"**
>
> ECCLESIASTES 4:9-11

There is also the blessing of fruitfulness and multiplication. When a man finds a good woman, he can start a family and have children. Together, they multiply, become fruitful and enjoy a continuation of their lineage.

> "Your wife will be like a fruitful grapevine, flourishing within your home. Your children will be like vigorous young olive trees as they sit around your table."
>
> PSALM 128:3

> "Children are a gift from the LORD; they are a reward from him."
>
> PSALM 127:3

The Bible recommends not just any woman but a good woman. This is a woman who loves and fears God, a godly and righteous person. So, the choice of a good woman is vital to living a happy life, which is why the Bible says, a man who finds a virtuous woman has the favour of God.

An ungodly woman with no fear of God, wisdom, love, or regard for other people will become a bad spouse which can create more problems than good for her husband. So, only a good and godly woman will bring blessing and provide an advantage for a man's progress and prosperity in life.

A foolish woman is usually irresponsible and will not care for her family. She will live a carefree and reckless life leading to the destruction of her home. Such a woman usually fights, and her nagging can cause her husband and the entire household to lose their peace and happiness.

> "It is better to live in a corner of the housetop [on the flat roof, exposed to the weather] Than in a house shared with a quarrelsome (contentious) woman."
>
> PROVERBS 21:9

> "The wise woman builds her house [on a foundation of godly precepts, and her household thrives], But the foolish one [who lacks spiritual insight] tears it down with her own hands [by ignoring godly principles]."
>
> PROVERBS 14:1

The success of a man can, therefore, depend upon the personality and choice of the wife that he marries. It is of utmost importance, for a man to ask the Lord in prayer for a prudent wife before asking any woman for her hand in marriage. There is an adage that says behind a successful man, there is a woman, the wisdom is to seek God for a good partner to do life with.

> **"Fathers can give their sons an inheritance of houses and wealth, but only the LORD can give an understanding wife."**
>
> PROVERBS 19:14

It must be said that the same principles apply to male partners. A contentious, quarrelsome man will also be difficult to live peacefully with, so, women ought to seek God's face in prayer before saying I do in marriage.

PRAYER

Father, we pray for young people both sons and daughters, and we ask that they find great and godly partners to marry and do life with, in Jesus' name. Amen.

CHAPTER 62

Oversleep and Poverty

> "Do not love [excessive] sleep, or you will become poor; Open your eyes [so that you can do your work] and you will be satisfied with bread."
>
> PROVERBS 20:13

The wisdom nugget is not to oversleep because excessive sleep will result in poverty. As aforementioned in previous chapters, the Bible warms the Believer not to oversleep because too much sleep is laziness. However, it must be said that insufficient sleep can hurt people's behavioural mood and cognition. So, there is a need to have a balanced sleep pattern and an appropriate time allocated for sleep.

Sleep is necessary for human beings because sleep is a valuable time to rest and refresh the body. During sleep, the cells revitalise and grow, whilst the brain recharges itself, and the body removes toxins and maintains the immune system. It is a time to recharge and recalibrate the human system. Sleep is vital for maintaining brain function and for optimising cognition for wellness.

A balanced quantity and quality of sleep are essential to provide human beings with daily energy and general vitality and performance. Insufficient, or excessive sleep harm human performance.

Overindulgence in sleep will lead to a negative habitual sleep pattern contrary to the acceptable standard recommended for successful living. Overall, too much sleep will contribute to the decline of cognitive performance.

Research has suggested an average of six to eight hours of sleep per 24 hours, usually taken during the night, for optimal well-being except in exceptional cases such as illnesses or other situations. There should be a set time for sleep and work, otherwise, the Bible says a person will become poor.

There are no fast rules for sleep patterns, each person should discover and work out what works for them, according to the nature and timing of their job, business, or life circumstances. The wisdom nugget is, therefore, to allocate a reasonable amount of time to sleep, set a specific time for sleep and have a balanced sleep and work pattern.

Believers ought to apply this godly and scientific guidance to their lives to prevent inadequate or excessive sleep. As the Bible says, too much sleep is laziness, and it leads to poverty and failure.

> **"A little extra sleep, a little more slumber, a little folding of the hands to rest, then poverty will pounce on you like a bandit; scarcity will attack you like an armed robber."**
>
> PROVERBS 6:10-11

> **"Laziness casts one into a deep sleep [unmindful of lost opportunity], And the idle person will suffer hunger."**
>
> PROVERBS 19:15

PRAYER

Dear Lord, we ask for the strength to develop a clever work and sleep-life balance to succeed and prosper in Jesus' name. Amen.

CHAPTER 63

Hold on to Collateral on Loans

> *"Get security from someone who guarantees a stranger's debt. Get a deposit if he does it for foreigners."*
>
> PROVERBS 27:13

The wisdom nugget is to ask for collateral from the borrower when lending money to people. Collateral is something pledged as security for repayment of a loan, forfeited in the event of a default. This is a form of guarantee or insurance just in case the borrower cannot pay the debt. It gives the creditor power to repossess the object of the collateral.

An illustration in the Bible is the story of the Prophet's wife whose husband died, leaving her in debt. The creditor took her sons as guarantors to pay the debt.

> "Now one of the wives *of a man* of the sons of the prophets cried out to Elisha [for help], saying "Your servant my husband is dead, and you know that your servant [reverently] feared the LORD, but the creditor is coming to take my two sons to be his slaves [in payment for a loan]."
>
> 2 KINGS 4:1

Collateral gives the creditor power over the borrower. The fact that the creditor has power over the debtor is a good reason for Christians to avoid borrowing or acting as a guarantor for other people's debt. Since creditors have the power, they can force the guarantor to pay for the debt on behalf of the borrower even though it is not their debt.

> **"He who puts up security *and* guarantees a debt for an outsider will surely suffer [for his foolishness], But he who hates (declines) being a guarantor is secure [from its penalties]."**
>
> PROVERBS 11:15

The lesson is to obtain valuable collateral if one decides to lend to other people. Collateral prevents bad debt and gives the guarantee that unpaid debt will be recovered through the object pledged as the security for the loan.

The ultimate wisdom is to abstain from unnecessary borrowings that do not generate income and not to act as the guarantor for loans or other people's borrowings.

PRAYER

O Lord, we pray for the wisdom to manage financial affairs wisely, to avoid financial misfortune, in Jesus' name. Amen.

CHAPTER 64

Do Honest Work – Stealing and Fraud Has Consequences

> "Food gained by fraud tastes sweet, but one ends up with a mouth full of gravel."
>
> PROVERBS 20:17

This wisdom nugget addresses theft and corrects those who steal for a living. It teaches Believers not to engage in crime in exchange for money. It encourages an honest living through work and business because theft will eventually have the consequence of punishment for the thief when caught.

> "People do not despise a thief if he steals to satisfy himself when he is hungry; But when he is found, he must repay seven times [what he stole]; He must give all the property of his house [if necessary to meet his fine]."
>
> PROVERBS 6:30-31

Christians should not become thieves who rob other people to earn a living or commit fraud to become rich. Furthermore, Believers in God should not become scammers who defraud people of their money or asset to earn a living. The right way for the people of God is to earn an honest living, exchanging their skills and talents for wages and profits through the methods of jobs, business, and investments.

It is God who gives his people their daily bread, Jesus teaches Christians to ask God for their daily bread in the place of prayer (Matthew 6). The empowerment and the blessing to gain wealth comes from God Almighty who is Jehovah Jireh the provider, El Shaddai, the all-sufficient God.

It should be emphasised that earning a living through deceitful and fraudulent ways is evil and wrong and the Bible says it ends up as gravel in the mouth. It is not the intended way that God wants his people to live financially. Fraudsters, swindlers, tricksters, quacks, thieves, robbers, scammers, and cheats are all going through the easy and wide financial gate which leads to destruction.

Stealing may generate a quick wealth, but it brings sorrows and regrets because it enriches only temporarily with punishment in the end. There are consequences to bear because justice usually catches up with thieves and eventually, thieves will receive the right punishment for their financial crimes.

Therefore, the right way to do life financially is to earn an honest living through a profitable business or a paid job. An honest day of work offers the Believer happiness and peace of mind. Christians should, therefore, pray for their provision. The Bible records prayer requests for provision.

> **"First, help me never to tell a lie. Second, give me neither poverty nor riches! Give me just enough to satisfy my needs. For if I grow rich, I may deny you and say, "Who is the LORD?" And if I am too poor, I may steal and thus insult God's holy name."**
>
> PROVERBS 30:8-9

"And this same God who takes care of me will supply all your needs from his glorious riches, which have been given to us in Christ Jesus."

PHILIPPIANS 4:19

PRAYER

O Lord, we pray for divine provision, we ask that you meet all our needs according to your glorious riches in Jesus' name. Amen.

CHAPTER 65

Planning, Expert Advice and Alliances

> "Plans succeed through good counsel; don't go to war without wise advice."
>
> PROVERBS 20:18

The wisdom nugget is to have a clear purpose and to seek good advice to generate the plans to accomplish them. And having set goals and creating useful alliances to help implement them. Plans are a detailed proposal for implementing a vision, it can be a series of methods created for achieving something. It requires wisdom and God's guidance to create a successful plan. The lesson is to seek God's divine purpose for one's life and seek divine destiny helpers and counsellors to make them happen.

The Bible advises the people of God to create and decide on the course of action to take for a successful life. The plan should be based upon wise counsel, devised by consultation with wise counsellors, that is, those who have insight, skill, and experience in the specific areas of pursuit. Counsel is the knowledge obtained from God, through the revelation of the Holy Spirit or the word of God, wise people, books, and online research.

Professionals and experts can also provide useful information and data required for creating plans and setting the goals to attain them. Thereby implementing one's vision for a successful life. In addition to getting the expertise required to successfully implement a vision, the Bible advises Christians to seek all the help and assistance they can get to implement their goals in life. Creating alliances and partnerships with like-minded people who have common goals and who are pursuing similar agendas and visions in life is a creative way to accomplish goals and plans.

In other words, creating teamwork with other people of good intention, direction and skill will empower the Believer to climb up and succeed faster. The lesson is that Believers should live a purposeful life by seeking God's purpose for their lives and pursuing such purpose with help from God and other great minds. The principle of power and safety in the multitude of counsellors (Proverbs 11:14), applies to fulfilling purpose and making a difference in life.

PRAYER

Dear Lord, we pray for divine helpers and counsellors who can empower us to accomplish purpose in Jesus' name. Amen.

CHAPTER 66

Secrets and Confidentiality

> "He who goes about as a gossip reveals secrets; Therefore, do not associate with a gossip [who talks freely or flatters]."
>
> PROVERBS 20:19

The wisdom nugget is to protect your secrets and confidential information. Do not release important matters and information to gossips or unsafe sources because they will share your secrets with people without your permission. Leviticus 19:16 warns Believers not to spread slander because it can endanger the life of their neighbour. Therefore, Believers should learn the art of confidentiality and keep information entrusted to them private.

Believers should refrain from confiding in those who gossip because they cannot keep secrets. Christians ought to guard their mouth and keep away from the bad influences of those who gossip. However, tempting juicy gossip may be, Christians should uphold their integrity and not become undependable talebearers whom people cannot trust with confidential matters or information.

The Bible says the word of the talebearer can be devastating to people's emotional well-being and peace. Maintaining confidentiality is, therefore, a peaceful way to live because one will prevent unnecessary strife and quarrels.

"A gossip reveals a secret, but a trustworthy person keeps confidence."

PROVERBS 11:13

"He who guards his mouth protects his life, but the one who opens his lips invites his ruin."

PROVERBS 13:3

"The words of a talebearer *are* as wounds, and they go down into the innermost parts of the bell"

PROVERBS 18:8

The lesson is to watch one's mouth and not be careless with other people's sensitive information or secrets. Christians should carefully select the friends to trust with secrets and confidential matters.

PRAYER

O Lord, we thank you for your wisdom in maintaining confidentiality. Teach us to know whom to trust with secrets and whom to confide in. Help us not to be a blabbermouth who cannot keep other people's secrets in Jesus' name. Amen.

CHAPTER 67

Honour Your Parents

> *"Whoever curses his father or his mother, his lamp [of life] will be extinguished in time of darkness."*
>
> PROVERBS 20:20

Honouring parents is one of the ten commandments that God gave to his people through Moses. It is a command that carries a reward of long life or the consequence of short life for those who disobey.

> **"Honour (respect, obey, care for) your father and your mother, so that your days may be prolonged in the land the LORD your God gives you."**
>
> EXODUS 20:12

> **"For instance, God says, 'Honour your father and mother,' and 'Anyone who speaks disrespectfully of father or mother must be put to death.'**
>
> MATTHEW 15:4

The wisdom nugget is, therefore, for children to respect and honour their parents and never to disrespect or curse them. God promise reward or consequences for children who mistreat their parents. He can stop their favour to breakthrough and succeed. It is important to note, that there is no excuse or any exceptional case to this law. Even if one has difficult parents, one will have to find a creative way to fulfil one's duty to them. Children should ensure they respect and take care of their parents to their best ability.

PRAYER

Dear Lord, we thank you for children and parents' relationships. We pray for your grace upon children to love and honour their parents in Jesus' name. Amen.

CHAPTER 68

Divine Direction and God's Guidance

> "Man's steps are ordered and ordained by the LORD. How then can a man [fully] understand his way?"
>
> PROVERBS 20:24

The wisdom nugget is to trust God's leading because he is a good shepherd who directs the steps of the upright. Steps are usually the plans, goals, and actions a person takes to progress and attain success in their life. It is the direction of a person, guarded by God whenever a person commits his ways to him. The Bible states human heart always device various plans but only the plans and aspirations submitted to God in alignment with his will and purpose will succeed.

Therefore, Christians are to do life asking daily in prayer for the divine guidance of God. God is a counsellor and a shepherd, he guides, orders, and directs the steps and the activities of his people. The Bible says God orders the steps of his people; this means, he is a good shepherd that guides and blesses his people with divine direction.

> "The step of a [good and righteous] man is directed *and* established by the LORD, And He delights in his way [and blesses his path]."
>
> PSALM 37:23

It is God who directs a person's course in life, he also establishes the steps of those who love him and commit themselves to obey his commandments. He is the good shepherd who leads and guides his people according to the Psalmist in Psalm 23.

> "A Psalm of David. The LORD is my Shepherd [to feed, to guide and to shield me], I shall not want. He lets me lie down in green pastures; He leads me beside the still *and* quiet waters. He refreshes *and* restores my soul (life); He leads me in the paths of righteousness for His name's sake."
>
> PSALM 23:1-3

Christians can pray for divine direction; the Bible records such prayer requests. Without the leadership of God, the Believer cannot successfully journey through life.

> "A man's mind plans his way [as he journeys through life], But the LORD directs his steps *and* establishes them."
>
> PROVERBS 16:9

> "Let me know Your ways, O LORD; Teach me Your paths. Guide me in Your truth and teach me, For You are the God of my salvation; For You [and only You] I wait [expectantly] all day long."
>
> PSALM 25:4-5

> "Teach me how to live, O LORD. Lead me along the right path, for my enemies are waiting for me."
>
> PSALM 27:11

Moses prayed for guidance and God helped and directed his path and that of the Israelites in their journey through the wilderness.

> "Now, therefore, I pray you, if I have found favour in Your sight, let me know Your ways so that I may know You [becoming more deeply and intimately acquainted with You, recognising, and understanding Your ways more clearly] and that I may find grace *and* favour in Your sight. And consider also, that this nation is Your people.
>
> And the LORD said, "My presence shall go *with you,* and I will give you rest [by bringing you and the people into the promised land]."
>
> EXODUS 33:13-14

PRAYER

O Lord, we pray that you teach us your ways and show us the divine direction for our lives in Jesus' name. Amen.

CHAPTER 69

Preparation and Victory

> "The horse is prepared for the day of battle, but deliverance and victory belong to the LORD."
>
> PROVERBS 21:31

The wisdom nugget is preparedness, God wants his people to do their best and be always prepared for whatever life may bring their way, whether opportunities or challenges. This requires Christians to diligently take necessary actions to prepare for opportunities and unforeseeable circumstances of life.

A horse is prepared and ready for war, they do not prepare when the war begins but way before it happens. Believers should therefore develop future-proof skills and have resources such as emergency funds and strategies for overcoming the challenges of life. However, Christians should acknowledge that regardless of their preparation for unforeseen circumstances, it is God that makes life secure.

The lesson is to trust God to give victory supernaturally. Whilst the Believer must do their best and prepare diligently, they must be dependent on God and not their strength or preparation. The Psalmist wrote that certain people, may trust in chariots, but Christians should trust in their God.

> "Some nations boast of their chariots and horses, but we boast in the name of the LORD our God."
>
> PSALM 20:7

The Believer should embrace the fact that it is God who delivers, provides, and protects his people. They should, therefore, put in their best efforts for their future success and security and leave the rest to God. The Bible says God is the author and finisher of our faith so Christians should look up to God and not depend solely on their power and strength.

> "Woe (judgment is coming) to those who go down to Egypt for help, who rely on horses and trust in chariots because they are many, and in horsemen, because they are very strong, but they do not look to the Holy One of Israel, nor seek *and* consult the LORD!"
>
> ISAIAH 31:1

> "We do this by keeping our eyes on Jesus, the champion who initiates and perfects our faith. Because of the joy awaiting him, he endured the cross, disregarding its shame. Now he is seated in the place of honour beside God's throne."
>
> HEBREWS 12:2

Apostle Paul wrote that the Believer should do their best and having done all to stand in anticipation of God granting them victory (Ephesians 6). He also emphasised that it is God who gives increase and crowns Christians endeavours with increase and success.

> "So, neither is the one who plants nor the one who waters anything, but [only] God who causes the growth."
>
> 1 CORINTHIANS 3:7

PRAYER

Heavenly Father, we pray for the ability, knowledge, and wisdom to prepare for the future, especially for unforeseeable circumstances. We ask that you help us to always do our best with the grace to trust you completely in Jesus' name. Amen.

CHAPTER 70

Be Skilled at Your Work, Skilled Workers are Always in Demand

> "Do you see a man skilful and experienced in his work? He will stand [in honour] before kings; He will not stand before obscure men."
>
> PROVERBS 22:29

The wisdom nugget is to get trained. Success requires Believers to acquire knowledge and skills to develop an excellent career or business. There is great admiration for those who are knowledgeable and skilled in their profession. The Bible promises work for talented people, they are presented with good opportunities and highly paid jobs, amidst great, generous, and influential people.

Great people are outstanding employers who are willing to pay an excellent salary in exchange for labour or desirable customers who are willing to pay decent prices that bring profits in exchange for goods and services. Whichever way one earns a living, whether in business or career, having extraordinary talent and skills is essential. Skilled workers are truly in demand.

So, the lesson is to know your game and develop your skill through education and training, which are readily available through schools and colleges, books, and online courses. However, it is useful to mention the need to take training to an excellent level to become a successful key person of influence.

Having basic skills is usually inadequate, so, training to the highest standard of competency is desirable to become high performers. Becoming an expert in a specific industry is necessary to become recognised and distinguished in life.

Competency is the key to being in demand, employers appreciate highly skilled people for leadership and managerial roles because they are capable and efficient in leading and motivating other people to achieve company goals. They are well driven, and they deliver exceptional performance in their work. They consistently outperform their colleagues and have excellent work ethics.

In the Bible time, efficient and talented people get work in palaces, working for Kings as highly positioned officials. Notable examples are Joseph and Jeroboam. Joseph got the job to manage the economy and resources of an entire nation, even though he was a foreigner in Egypt (Genesis 41:46). And Jeroboam became the armour bearer to King Solomon.

> **"Jeroboam was a very capable young man, and when Solomon saw how industrious he was, he put him in charge of the labour force from the tribes of Ephraim and Manasseh, the descendants of Joseph."**
>
> 1 KING 11:28

Diligence is vital to becoming successful, employers usually scout for highly skilled professionals for their corporation. God is the giver of skill and talent that human beings cultivate and develop to excellence. King Solomon showed the example that Believers can ask God for whatever is lacking in wisdom and talent to do life well. He prayed for wisdom to rule his people to become a successful king and ruler (1 Kings 3:9) and God granted his wishes and prayer requests.

God gives skills, abilities, and an excellent spirit to his people. He spoke in Exodus 31:3 that he has filled a man with the spirit of God, to have the skill, ability, and knowledge to design artistic works. Whilst God gives the talent, Believers must cultivate and use their talent for greatness. Christians ought to train themselves and acquire knowledge through books, apprenticeships, and formal education. There are consequences of poverty for those who fail to acquire useful skills and God punishes those who bury their talent.

The parable of the Talent expresses the disgust that God showed towards the lazy servant who buried his talent. He received the talent to multiply, but he hid it due to fear of failure and laziness, so, God punished him and called him wicked and lazy for failing to multiply or invest his talent. His one talent was taken away from him and given to the person who multiplied his five talents.

> "So, I was afraid [to lose the talent], and I went and hid your talent in the ground. See, you have what is your own. "But his master answered him, 'You wicked, lazy servant, you knew that I reap [the harvest] where I did not sow and gather where I did not scatter *seed*. Then you ought to have put my money with the bankers, and at my return, I would have received my *money* back with interest."
>
> MATTHEW 25:25-27

The lesson is to ask God for outstanding talent and skill, then, develop and use them to multiply, invest, and generate wealth.

PRAYER

Father, we ask for talent and skills to do life beautifully and successfully in Jesus' name. Amen.

CHAPTER 71

Do Not Wear Yourself Out Trying to Get Rich

> "Do not wear yourself out trying to get rich. Be wise enough to know when to quit. In the blink of an eye wealth disappears, for it will sprout wings and fly away like an eagle."
>
> PROVERBS 23:4-5

The wisdom nugget is to not focus too much on money at the expense of one's wellbeing. Christians ought not to be greedy or consumed with the desire to get rich at the expense of the prosperity of their soul and health. Toiling for money brings stress and causes damage to health. It can cause Believers to stumble in their path to righteousness.

Whilst this scripture is condemning Believers' attempts to get rich at all costs, it does not condemn riches sought by godly principles. Riches and wealth are the entitlement of those who love God and work according to godly financial principles and ethics. The Bible says God gives his people wealth without adding any pressure, stress, sorrow, regrets, temptation, or hardship to it. Therefore, the lesson of this scripture is not to pursue wealth at the expense of good health, well-being, and godly morals.

> **"The blessing of the LORD brings [true] riches and He adds no sorrow to it [for it comes as a blessing from God]"**
>
> PROVERBS 10:22

Riches obtained by fraudulent means, crime, toiling, stress, and cheating are unholy and will eventually bring pain and curses to a person. Timothy warned against the deceitfulness of riches at the expense of righteousness.

> **"But those who [are not financially ethical and] crave to get rich [with a compulsive, greedy longing for wealth] fall into temptation and a trap and into many foolish and harmful desires that plunge people into ruin and destruction [leading to personal misery]."**
>
> 1 TIMOTHY 6:9

Wisdom and contentment are the keys to a successful financial life. Therefore, developing excellent skills for working smart to earn a good living, whilst obeying God's commandment, and refuting greed and avarice, are the godly ways to gain true riches with no sorrow or hardship. After all, God is El Shaddai, the provider and source of all things, who supplies every need. He is Jehovah Jireh, who provides for his people. Apostle Paul said Christians should not be anxious about their financial needs, rather they should pray, trusting God for their provision.

> **"And my God will liberally supply (fill until full) your every need according to His riches in glory in Christ Jesus."**
>
> PHILIPPIANS 4:19

Christians should have good moral standards and endeavour to live an upright life financially, always living a life of integrity and honesty as per their finances.

> "Let your character [your moral essence, your inner nature] be free from the love of money [shun greed—be financially ethical], being content with what you have; for He has said, "I WILL NEVER [under any circumstances] DESERT YOU [nor give you up nor leave you without support, nor will I in any degree leave you helpless], NOR WILL I FORSAKE *or* LET YOU DOWN *or* RELAX MY HOLD ON YOU [assuredly not]!"
>
> HEBREWS 13:5

God wants his people to prosper and live an abundant life with an overflow of money and wealth to enjoy life without compromising their integrity and faith in God. Jesus Christ said his purpose is to give human beings a rich and satisfying life free of poverty and stress.

> "The thief's purpose is to steal and kill and destroy. My purpose is to give them a rich and satisfying life."
>
> JOHN 10:10

> "For you are recognizing [more clearly] the grace of our Lord Jesus Christ [His astonishing kindness, His generosity, His gracious favour], that though He was rich, yet for your sake, He became poor so that by His poverty you might become rich (abundantly blessed)."
>
> 2 CORINTHIANS 8:9

PRAYER

Father, we pray for the grace to live a motivated, yet contented life, without the urge to sacrifice moral ethics or health in exchange for money in Jesus' name. Amen.

CHAPTER 72

Moderation of Food and Wine

> *"Do not associate with heavy drinkers of wine, Or with gluttonous eaters of meat."*
>
> **PROVERBS 23:20**

The wisdom nugget is to eat moderately and avoid association with gluttons and drunkards. The Bible advice the people of God to avoid drunkards and gluttons because those who give to excessive drinking habits or overeating usually influence other people to join their unhealthy habits. There is a saying that bad company corrupts good nature.

> *"Do not be deceived: "Evil company corrupts good habits."*
>
> **1 CORINTHIANS 15:33**

Wine and food should be consumed moderately, Believers should not overindulge themselves in alcohol and food. Whilst, the Bible is not condemning food or alcohol, it is strongly against excessive consumption of food and drink because this can affect behaviour and character, leading to greed, gluttony, drunkenness, and obesity.

Jesus at a wedding in Cana performed the miracle of turning water into wine for the guests to enjoy (John 2:1-11). And Apostle Paul advised Timothy to take a little wine as a medicinal drink for his stomach pain (1 Timothy 5:23). These Bible stories confirm that alcohol and food are not the issues but excessive consumption of them. Excessive eating leads to greed and gluttony whilst too much alcohol will lead to drunkenness. The Bible teaches Christians to behave decently and do everything in moderation, this includes eating and drinking.

> **"Do not be drunk with wine because that will ruin your life. Instead, be filled with the Holy Spirit."**
>
> EPHESIANS 5:18

PRAYER

Father, we pray for the grace to do life in moderation. We ask for the strength to eat and drink in moderation and not to join drunkards and gluttons in their ways in Jesus' name. Amen.

CHAPTER 73

Intelligence and Wise Strategies

> *"The wise are mightier than the strong, and those with knowledge grow stronger and stronger."*
>
> PROVERBS 24:5

This wisdom nugget declares wisdom and intelligence are better than strength. There is an adage to not just work hard but be smart because brainpower outweighs muscle power. The Bible says victory is won by the wisdom of a multitude of counsellors (Proverbs 24:6). A wise man with insight, rescued his nation in the Bible, though, people forgot him because of his poverty, his wisdom saved his nation (Ecclesiastes 9:15).

The wisdom is to gain knowledge and wisdom and equip oneself with essential insight into affairs of life necessary to live smartly. What the Bible is teaching in this scripture is to employ strategic planning to win the race of life. Strategic planning is the core principle of success and effective planning requires intelligence and insight.

Strategic planning is the process of documenting and establishing steps and directions to accomplish vision and purpose. Wisdom and intelligence give the strength to know what to do (vision) and how to do them through actionable plans, goals, and missions.

Wisdom, therefore, is the motivating factor for living a successful life, not physical strength even though strength and stamina play a role in the development and implementation of wise plans.

PRAYER

Dear Lord, we ask for the wisdom and divine intelligence to live successfully in Jesus' name. Amen.

CHAPTER 74

Stay Upright – Do Not Compromise

> "Like a muddied fountain and a polluted spring Is a righteous man who yields and compromises his integrity before the wicked."
>
> PROVERBS 25:26

The wisdom nugget is to hold on to one's integrity and never to compromise or yield to corruption and bad influence from ungodly people. Psalm 1 teaches how to stay upright; the Psalmist advises the people of God not to keep the association with immoral people because of their negative influence on their character. The Bible says friendship with the world corrupts good character and behaviour.

Those who yield to sin lose their soul to the devil. The Bible warns there is no long-term profit for those who gain the world and its reward of money, fame, and power. There will be judgement, ruin, regret, and damnation to hell in the end for the wicked.

> "For whoever wishes to save his life [in this world] will [eventually] lose it [through death], but whoever loses his life [in this world] for my sake and the gospel's will save it [from the

consequences of sin and separation from God]. For what does it benefit a man to gain the whole world [with all its pleasures], and forfeit his soul? For what will a man give in exchange for his soul *and* eternal life [in God's kingdom]?"

MARK 8:35-37

Christians should, therefore, live a life of integrity and uphold righteousness, they ought to always pray and not faint and trust God for divine prosperity. Psalm 1 declares blessings upon those who keep God's law and delight in his ways.

PRAYER

Father, we thank you for your word, we pray for the strength to live uprightly and never to succumb to bad worldly influences. We pray for the grace to remain steadfast in righteousness in Jesus' name. Amen.

CHAPTER 75

Subdue Yourself – Self-Discipline

> *"Like a city that is broken down and without walls [leaving it unprotected] is a man who has no self-control over his spirit [and sets himself up for trouble]."*
>
> PROVERBS 25:28

The wisdom nugget is to have self-control. Self-Control is a fruit of the Holy Spirit, it means self-discipline which is the ability to control one's body and soul, taking control of human cravings and excessive appetite, temper, greed, avarice, lust, and negative emotions. It is being able to subdue the flesh to live a balanced life. A life of self-discipline will give Believers a positive outcome in life.

Therefore, Christians should learn to tame and have dominion over themselves, subduing the negative effects of greed which results in gluttony, over-drinking, and outburst of anger. Apostle Paul taught on how to prevent the emotion of anger from spinning out of control, by getting over it before sleeping.

"BE ANGRY [at sin—at immorality, at injustice, at ungodly behaviour], YET DO NOT SIN; do not let your anger [cause you shame, nor allow it to] last until the sun goes down."

EPHESIANS 4:26

PRAYER

O Lord, we pray for the grace of self-discipline. We ask for the manifestation of the fruit of the Holy Spirit, self-control in Jesus' name. Amen.

CHAPTER 76

Teamwork and Friendships

> "As iron sharpens iron, so, one man sharpens [and influences] another [through discussion]."
>
> PROVERBS 27:17

There is power in collective wisdom. The Bible says one will chase a thousand but two will put ten thousand to flight (Deuteronomy 32:20). This suggests it is better to work with others than to work alone. The wisdom nugget of Proverbs 27:17 is, therefore, to have quality people around with whom one can do relationships, through discussion of ideas to help synergise and expand one's thought.

There is power in teamwork and prayer of agreement for wealth generation and general well-being. Like-minded friendships help people create and build an enjoyable life. Having a network of wise and intelligent people promotes success because alliances propel people forward, and make progress happen faster than when one person works alone.

There is power in two! Jesus taught about the power in the prayer of agreement, this is based on the principle of mutual relationship and teamwork. Whenever two people come together in agreement to pray concerning anything, Jesus said they will get answers to their prayer requests (Matthew 18: 19). The Bible further declares that one person will chase one thousand but two people will put ten thousand to flight (Deuteronomy 32:30) That is an exponential increase, demonstrating the power of two people working together in agreement to do exploits.

PRAYER

Father, we ask for your guidance to create an alliance with the right people of like mind, that can help us to advance and make progress in our endeavours. We pray for the wisdom and emotional intelligence to develop excellent relationships and friendships with godly and intelligent people in Jesus' name. Amen.

CHAPTER 77

Vision, Purpose, and Revelation

> "Where there is no vision [no revelation of God and His word], the people are unrestrained; But happy and blessed is he who keeps the law [of God]."
>
> PROVERBS 29:18

The wisdom nugget is to have a vision which is the ability to see and know what to do in life. God gives purpose and direction for life, so the best way to receive vision is through revelations from his word and the Holy Spirit. Revelation is the enlightenment or disclosure of God's plans or will, divinely revealed to the human mind by God the Holy Spirit.

This scripture suggests a person without vision, cannot see, therefore, they will lack purpose and will not know what to do with their time. They go about aimlessly, trying all sorts of things that yield no profit. However, God helps his people to see. He sheds his light which is his word, the Bible unto their paths, guiding them and whispering to them the way to go.

God spoke to Abraham after Lot had departed from him telling him to lift his eyes to look to the land in all directions, for he has given the land to him and his descendants.

> "The LORD said to Abram after Lot had left him, "Now lift up your eyes and look from the place where you are *standing*, northward and southward and eastward and westward; for all the land which you see I will give to you and your descendants forever."
>
> GENESIS 13:14-15

God renewed his promise to Abraham and gave him a vision for the future. Vision helps people to see into the unforeseen future, to know what is to come for their destiny and to visualise the life that God has in store for them. The aim is to help the Believer plan and create goals to implement their desired life.

The Bible says people perish for lack of knowledge (Hosea 4:6) because of lack of knowledge and the vision for a good life they lose hope and live carelessly. However, with God's guidance and divine counsel, the Believer will do exploits. Some great questions to ask are, what life do you see? And what are you going to do about it?

Habakkuk instructed his readers to write their vision down so that whoever reads it can run with it and help them accomplish it through careful planning and divine strategies.

> "I will stand at my guard post and station myself on the tower; And I will keep watch to see what He will say to me, and what answer I will give [as His spokesman] when I am reproved. Then the LORD answered me and said, "Write the vision and engrave it plainly on [clay] tablets So that the one who reads it will run. For the vision is yet for the appointed [future] time It hurries toward the goal [of fulfilment]; it will not fail. Even though it delays, wait [patiently] for it, because it will certainly come; it will not delay."
>
> HABAKKUK 2:1-3

Notice Habakkuk waited on God in prayer, seeking him for the vision for the future, God gave him a vision and instructed him to document what he saw. So, whatever vision God gives to you, write it down for future implementation.

Businesses start with visionaries who receive vision and dreams, they write down their vision for the business in what is known as a business plan. Likewise, Christians ought to write down their vision for the life they desire. They should see themselves accomplishing their best life, that is, the woman or the man they want to become.

PRAYER

O Lord, we ask for a divine vision for our lives. Give us divine purpose and direction in Jesus' name. Amen.

CHAPTER 78

Humility Versus Pride

> "A man's pride and sense of self-importance will bring him down, but he who has a humble spirit will obtain honour."
>
> PROVERBS 29:23

The wisdom nugget is to be humble because as the Bible predicts, pride comes before a fall (Proverbs 16:18). However, it is important to distinguish a righteous humble spirit from false humility which is a pretentious sham that ungodly people use to deceive others into thinking they are humble. Genuine humility is having a reasonable estimation of one's worth and status. It is not arrogant self-importance condemned by the Bible.

> "For by the grace [of God] given to me I say to every one of you not to think more highly of himself [and of his importance and ability] than he ought to think; but to think to have sound judgment, as God has apportioned to each a degree of faith [and a purpose-designed for service]."
>
> ROMANS 12:3

Apostle Paul advised Christians not to be proud, but to practise godly humility which promotes peace and harmony in relationships.

> "Live in harmony with one another; do not be haughty [conceited, self-important, exclusive], but associate with humble people [those with a realistic self-view]. Do not overestimate yourself."
>
> ROMANS 12:16

Humility is not low self-esteem, lack of confidence or good self-image. It is simply appreciating other people and treating them as equals. Pride disregard people and look down on them, but humility treats people as important. Humble people live life with a healthy view of themselves and others, hence they get along well with people thereby maintaining great relationships.

Humble people are respectful and receptive to other people's ways of doing things, they accept alternative opinions and consider all views in their decision-making. They acknowledge other people's ideas and opinions, accepting they may be good or even better than theirs.

The previously mentioned parable of the Pharisee and the Tax Collector praying in the temple portrays the arrogance of a self-righteous Pharisee obsessed with self-righteousness compared with the humility of a tax collector who humbly asked God for mercy during prayer. The Pharisee boasted arrogantly about his virtue, Jesus said he went home condemned whilst the Tax Collector who humbled himself before God went home justified.

The Bible declares that God gives more grace to the humble and opposes the proud. Disgrace usually follows pride whilst humility comes with wisdom (Proverbs 11:2). Jesus when he noticed how the guests picked the places of honour at the table, told a parable to teach people how to behave at a feast.

He said when one is invited to a feast, one should take a low seat and not a place of honour because there may arrive someone more distinguished and the host may ask you to give up the seat for them. One will, therefore, accept the least prominent place in humiliation (Luke 14:9-11).

PRAYER

Dear Heavenly Father, we pray for the gift of meekness, teach us to be humble in Jesus' name. Amen.

CHAPTER 79

Managing Negative Criticisms

> *"Fearing people is a dangerous trap but trusting the LORD means safety."*
>
> PROVERBS 29:25

The wisdom nugget is not to be afraid of what people think. Do not care about what people think because opinions change and only God's approval matter. Human beings have feeble minds; therefore, their opinions change according to their moods, perception, mindsets, peer pressure, emotions, environmental influences, and financial motives.

People can praise a person one day and curse them another day. There are numerous examples in the Bible where the Israelites sing praises of their leaders when things go well but curse and stone them when things go wrong. It is, therefore, wise to take peoples' praises with a pinch of salt and to ignore their negative criticism which can derail destinies.

Having a vision and staying focused, treating negative criticisms as distractions is the best way to forge ahead to achieve one's God-given destiny. Luke 12:4 advises Christians not to be afraid of people. James teaches not to seek the praise of people but the approval of God (John 12:43).

When one is attentive mainly to God's leading, human opinions become irrelevant, not central or paramount to successful living. Believers should therefore delight themselves in God and follow the example of Jesus Christ who lived only to please God and the Bible confirmed God the Father was pleased with him.

> "And behold, a voice from heaven said, "This is My beloved Son, in whom I am well-pleased *and* delighted!"
>
> MATTHEW 3:17

PRAYER

Lord, we pray for the strength to trust in you, we ask for the will to ignore criticisms and negative opinions of people in Jesus' name. Amen.

CHAPTER 80

Get Rid of Negative Emotions

> "As the beating of cream yields butter and striking the nose causes bleeding, so stirring up anger causes quarrels."
>
> PROVERBS 30:33

The wisdom nugget is to get rid of negative emotions of anger, upsets, and bitterness of the soul. Unresolved anger causes bitterness that will eventually turn into fights or quarrels. The wisdom for successful living is therefore forgiveness, do not harbour grudges, get rid of anger and bitterness quickly and forgive those who offend you. Apostle Paul advises Christians to make effort to pursue peace and to live a holy life making allowances for offences and getting rid of anger and resentments quickly to avoid escalation into fights.

> "Make every effort to live in peace with everyone and to be holy; without holiness, no one will see the Lord. See to it that no one falls short of the grace of God and that no bitter root grows up to cause trouble and defile many."
>
> HEBREWS 12:14-15

> "Bearing graciously with one another, and willingly forgiving each other if one has a cause for complaint against another; just as the Lord has forgiven you, so should you forgive."
>
> COLOSSIANS 3:13

Walking in love and cultivating a habit of forgiveness will help Christians overcome riled emotions. The benefits are a happy, peaceful, and healthy life. Jesus taught his disciples to offer limitless forgiveness to their friends and family who offend them (Matthew 18:21-22).

Prayer is another way to live a sweet and delightful life. When we go to God in prayer, we must forgive others so that our Father in heaven can forgive us our offenses too. Prayer, therefore, offers Christians the opportunity to empty negative emotions such as resentments, anger, and bitterness in exchange for peace of mind and a sweet spirit.

> 'And forgive us our debts, as we have forgiven our debtors [letting go of both the wrong and the resentment]."
>
> MATTHEW 6:12

PRAYER

Dear Lord, we pray for a clean and pure heart, a heart free of resentments which can cause pain in our relationships. Father, grant us the gift of patience and the grace to forbear in Jesus' name. Amen.

CHAPTER 81

An Excellent Wife

> "An excellent woman [one who is spiritual, capable, intelligent, and virtuous], who is he who can find her? Her value is more precious than jewels and her worth is far above rubies or pearls."
>
> PROVERBS 31:10

A good wife is a virtuous and capable woman. A woman who is upright spiritually, emotionally, physically, and financially. The Bible says it takes the grace of God to find such a woman because they are rare. Proverbs 31:10 explains that she is godly, knows the Lord and passionately serves God. She is highly skilled, industrious, intelligent, and smart. She has a good moral standard, and she is virtuous. Proverbs 31 says she is worthy of praise and accolade.

The Wife of Noble Character

"A good woman is hard to find and worth far more than diamonds. Her husband trusts her without reserve and never has reason to regret it. Never spiteful, she treats him generously all her life long. She shops around for the best yarns and cotton and enjoys knitting and sewing. She is like a trading ship that sails to faraway places and brings back exotic surprises. She is up before dawn, preparing breakfast for her family and organizing her day. She looks over a field and buys it, then, with money she has put aside, plants a garden. First thing in the morning, she dresses for work, rolls up her sleeves, eager to start. She senses the worth of her work and is in no hurry to call it quits for the day. She is skilled in the crafts of home and hearth and diligent in homemaking. She is quick to assist anyone in need and reaches out to help the poor. She does not worry about her family when it snows; their winter clothes are all mended and ready to wear. She makes her clothing and dresses in colourful linens and silks. Her husband is respected when he deliberates with the city leaders. She designs gowns and sells them; brings the sweaters she knits to the dress shops. Her clothes are well-made and elegant, and she always faces tomorrow with a smile. When she speaks, she has something worthwhile to say, and she always says it kindly. She keeps an eye on everyone in her household and keeps them all busy and productive. Her children respect and bless her; her husband joins in with words of praise: "Many women have done wonderful things, but you've outclassed them all!" Charm can mislead and beauty soon fades. The woman to be admired and praised is the woman who lives in the Fear-of-God. Give her everything she deserves! Festoon her life with praises!"

PROVERBS 31:10-31

The preceding scriptures list the qualities of a good wife which include the following characteristics that demonstrate her excellency and skill sets.

The Qualities of a Good Wife

- She is hospitable; she cooks for her family
- She is well organised; she organises her day well
- She is an investor; she buys land and businesses

- She is resourceful; she manages her money well
- She is pleasant and gentle; she is not spiteful
- She is hardworking; she works smartly and is very industrious
- She is an astute businesswoman; she trades and engages in business
- She is a homemaker; she builds a happy and content home
- She is not lazy; she wakes up early in the morning and never oversleeps
- She is frugal and economical; she shops around for bargains
- She is a good time manager; she manages time well
- She is a strong woman; she has confidence and strength
- She is diligent and skilled; she has an excellent spirit
- She is prosperous; she provides for her family
- She is prudent; she does whatever her hands find to do with prudence
- She is trustworthy; she makes her husband secure and happy
- She is lovable; she gets her husband's affection and esteem
- She is competent; she is never idle; she has a side hustle
- She is creative; she plants a garden of vegetables and flowers
- She is helpful; she helps other people
- She is charitable; she helps her fellow human beings
- She is generous; she gives and helps the poor
- She is smart and elegant; her character is upright
- She is God-fearing; she loves God wholeheartedly
- She is caring; she keeps an eye out for everyone in her household
- She is a leader and mentor; she guides and leads others
- She is a good manager; she manages her household well, making sure everyone is productive and engaged in work
- She is brave; she manages life challenges well
- She is optimistic; she cheerfully faces each day with a smile
- She is wise; she offers wisdom and kind words to people
- She is compassionate; she shows people kindness
- She is a blessing; her community recognise her contribution
- She is favoured; she outclasses other women

- She is honourable; she earns respect and love
- She is godly; she lives righteously
- She is blessed by God and man; her children call her blessed
- She is praiseworthy; her husband and children praise her
- She is anointed; God anoints her for wealth and excellence

The good wife is of great worth indeed! Her character is excellent, she is a distinguished role model for Christians. However, it is necessary to mention, that this woman did not get to become this wonderful person all by her power.

The Bible states she fears God, so, automatically, she possesses God's divine help to become the woman she is. God anoints her; hence, she enjoys the empowerment of God to live life beautifully, the way she does. One can, therefore, conclude that her unique quality or her secret for being who she is, must be her love and passion for God with whom all things are possible. God, therefore, is her secret, so every woman who trusts God can become a good wife if they so desire.

PRAYER

Father, we pray for women all over the world, we ask that you give an excellent spirit like that of the Proverbs 31 woman to any woman who desires to become an excellent wife. We pray for the empowerment of the Holy Spirit and the favour of God upon such women. Lord, help them to become godly, capable, excellent, and virtuous wives if they so desire to become one in Jesus' name. Amen.

CONCLUSION
TRUE PROSPERITY

> "Beloved, I wish above all things that thou may prosper and be in health, even as thy soul prospers"
>
> 3 JOHN 1:2

Whilst this book is for the spiritual, and physical prosperity of Christians, the wisdom nuggets will work for anyone who follows the principles. The word of God works for any human being who obeys the instructions because God is not a respecter of persons. God is love and his love abounds towards all of humanity. He will bless whoever reaches out to him for his blessing.

However, there is an exception to the rule. Whilst following the rules will physically prosper anyone who follows the principles, the human soul requires an acceptance of Jesus Christ as Lord to prosper spiritually. The Bible teaches that except a person accepts the son of God Jesus Christ as the Messiah, and lives a life of obedience to his commandments, they will not be able to enjoy eternal life after death.

Therefore, the word of God, the Bible will only work for the physical success and prosperity of those who do not accept Christ, but it will not work for their salvation or the prosperity of their soul for salvation and eternal life. Their success, therefore, is temporal according to Apostle Paul. It is better to focus on unseen things that are permanent.

> "So, we look not at the things which are seen, but at the things which are unseen; for the things which are visible are temporal [just brief and fleeting], but the things which are invisible are everlasting *and* imperishable."
>
> 2 CORINTHIANS 4:18

To qualify and enjoy spiritual prosperity after death, therefore, one must surrender their will to God, and believe in and accept Jesus Christ as the Lord and Saviour of the world. The next page contains the prayer to become a born Christian, being born again means asking the Lord Jesus into one's heart and doing life together with him. That way, one will have the prosperity of body, soul, and spirit, with the potential to enjoy this world's abundance and readiness for eternal life with God in heaven.

PRAYER

O Lord, we pray for the blessing of God that adds no sorrow, the fullness of life with salvation and the grace to live life abundantly for every reader in Jesus' name. Amen.

ALTAR CALL
PRAYER OF SALVATION

> *"For God so loved the world that he gave his one and only Son, that whoever believes in him shall not perish but have eternal life."*
>
> JOHN 3:16

An altar call is an invitation to those who wish to make a new spiritual commitment to Jesus Christ the Saviour and become a born-again Christian through a prayer of repentance and confession of sin and acceptance of Jesus Christ as their Lord and Saviour.

Prayer of Salvation, Author's Version

If you would like to know Jesus as your saviour and sanctifier, say this prayer:

> **"Dear Lord Jesus, I believe in my heart that you are the Messiah, the son of God who has come in the flesh and has lived, died, and resurrected for my sin. I ask for forgiveness of sin in your name, I confess with my mouth that Jesus is Lord. I ask that you come and dwell in my heart. I ask for the fruit and gift of the Holy Spirit with the evidence of speaking in tongues and the joy of your salvation in Jesus' name. Amen."**

Congratulations you are now a Born-Again Christian!

Welcome Letter to new Christians

Hey guys,

Welcome to the Kingdom of God, please know that God loves you and has a plan for your life. Below are a few tips for a successful Christian life.

New Christian To-Do List:

- Do get yourself a Bible to read and study the word of God
- Find a Bible-Believing Church to attend and fellowship for a successful life as a new-born-again Christian
- God loves you; He has a plan and a purpose for your life
- Discover and fulfil your purpose, then, have influence and make a difference in the world.

Best wishes in your new Christian walk with God!

PRAYER

Father Lord, we thank you for the new Christians that have just come into the Kingdom of God. We ask that you walk with them, be with them and help them make progress in their Christian journey in Jesus' name. Amen.

ABOUT THE AUTHOR

Caroline Bimbo Afolalu is a Christian, devoted to God and prayers. She has been a Christian since childhood but officially gave her life to the Lord Jesus Christ in the summer of 1986 at a Christian crusade in Akure, Nigeria, West Africa before migrating to the United Kingdom in 1992.

Caroline works as a company director with a demonstrated history of working in the food production industry since 2001. She is the founder and director of Beautiful Foods Ltd the owner of Tabitha's brand of Chin Chin, a West African Nigerian Snack operating in London UK.

Caroline is married to Tunde Afolalu since September 1992, they have, three wonderful and successful children - Adebisi, Pelumi, and Grace Ife Afolalu.

Caroline believes in marketplace ministry. She runs a daily prayer and teaching YouTube channel (Prayer Nuggets) and Tabitha's Charity with a focus on village women in Nigerian villages, alongside running her food manufacturing business in the United Kingdom.

Caroline would like to simply be known as Mrs Caroline Bimbo Afolalu the great! Achieving greatness in the simplest ways as a daughter, wife, mother, businessperson, and woman of God.

OTHER BOOKS BY THE AUTHOR

- How to Start a Business - A Guide to Starting and Growing a Food Business
- Beautiful Foods - The Art of African Catering
- The Names of God – How to Pray with God's names
- Prayer Nuggets - Inspiring Prayer Journal

Upcoming Books

- The Promised Life - Wisdom Nuggets from Joshua

CONTACT DETAILS

Websites

Work
www.beautifulfoods.co.uk
www.tabithaschinchin.com

Charity
www.prayernuggets.com

WORKS CITED

The Holy Bible

New International Version, New Living Translation,

English standard version, Berean Study Bible, King James Bible, World English Bible, New American Bible, New King James Version.

RECOMMENDED RESOURCES

The Holy Bible

www.ingramcontent.com/pod-product-compliance
Lightning Source LLC
Chambersburg PA
CBHW071903290426
44110CB00013B/1257